The Flexible Investing Playbook

ASSET ALLOCATION STRATEGIES FOR LONG-TERM SUCCESS

Robert A. Isbitts

WILEY

John Wiley & Sons, Inc.

Published by John Wiley & Sons, Inc., Hoboken, New Jersey.
Published simultaneously in Canada.

For general information on our other products and services or for technical support, please contact our Customer Care Department within the United States at (800) 762-2974, outside the United States at (317) 572-3993 or fax (317) 572-4002.

Wiley also publishes its books in a variety of electronic formats. Some content that appears in print may not be available in electronic books. For more information about Wiley products, visit our web site at www.wiley.com.

Library of Congress Cataloging-in-Publication Data:

Isbitts, Robert A.
  The flexible investing playbook: asset allocation strategies for long-term success/ Robert A. Isbitts.
    p. cm.
  Includes index.
  ISBN 978-0-470-63616-9 (cloth); 978-0-470-87556-8 (ebk); 978-0-470-87555-1 (ebk)
  1. Investments. 2. Securities. 3. Finance, Personal. I. Title.
  HG4521.I83 2010
  332.6—dc22

                                                      2010008454

Printed in the United States of America

10 9 8 7 6 5 4 3 2 1

To Dana, Jordann, Tyler, and Morgan Isbitts.
Everything I do, I do for you.

Contents

Acknowledgments

There are so many people who have influenced the thoughts and opinions that led to the creation of this book. First, there are the investors and financial advisors who had the courage to be early adopters of my investment philosophy. Now that this genre of investing has matured from a set of basic ideas into a formalized, sustainable, investment process, those who have come along for the ride have been rewarded for their patience.

The mutual fund managers whose investment styles piqued my curiosity starting in the mid-1990s were the true inspiration for this book. Just as a good team coach needs to effectively use his players and put them in positions to help the team win, so it is with the outstanding and innovative fund managers I have had the pleasure to spend time with over the years. They do the day-to-day security selection, and I use my strategic approach to determine how to set and maintain the team's "lineup." Mutual funds have been around since 1924 and I don't see them going away anytime soon. Thus, I am excited about the prospect of finding additional funds to blend into the portfolios for the next many years.

My parents, Joyce and Carl Isbitts, are the ones who instilled in me the discipline, energy, and persistence to make the concept of Flexible Investing a reality. I owe my inner strength to them.

My brother Mark and his family, while many miles away, have been a constant reminder that one's support network and family bond is more important than any financial victory or defeat.

My in-laws, Max and Vicki Rosen, transcend (nearly) every stereotype about "in-laws." They have been among my biggest fans, and they have completed the family picture that provides the backbone for all great ideas.

My aunt and uncle, Myrna and Paul Fruitt, and cousins Lisa Fruitt, Gary Markowitz, and Sid Krex have taught me so much and have been longtime supporters of the goals and dreams that are described in this book. I can truly say that when it comes to family, I don't have quantity, but boy do I have quality!

John Lohr, my mentor in the writing business, shares the accolades for this book. My first book, *Wall Street's Bull and How to Bear It* was published by John's publishing company, Isle Press in 2006. Before and since that time, John's perspective on the investment management business has been both thought-stimulating and very enjoyable. He is one of the unsung heroes of fair play in the investment business, and I am grateful for having the opportunity to know him.

My career has had numerous twists and turns and at each bend, I accumulated some knowledge and relationships that allowed me to eventually put together the "playbook" you are now reading. People like Donna Naitove, Scot Hunter, Allan Budelman, Medon Michaelides, Denise Karp, Pamela Nelson, and Leana Alu have all played a role in moving the process forward. In particular, I wish to thank those who have gone to battle alongside me in the day-to-day effort to uncover investment ideas and analyze their potential: Keith Stoloff, Michael Kahn, Suzie Dean, and Matthew MacEachern.

And most significantly, my wife Dana, and our three fantastic children have been the meaning behind everything I do. As any parent will tell you, one reaches a certain point in life where as much as you enjoy your professional accomplishments and free time, it just means more when you have your family there to share the joy with you. There is no shortage of that in our family, and I could not ask for anything more than I have at home. As a country song says, "the view I love the most is my front porch looking in."

INTRODUCTION

Replacing Your Old Investment Playbook

When a football player is cut from his team or traded to another team, his former team immediately asks him to turn in his "playbook," which shows diagrams of all the different ways his team will try to move the ball forward to score (if on offense) or how to defend when the other team has the ball. When the player arrives at his new team, one of the first things they give him is his new playbook. They ask him to go learn it. One reason why many rookie quarterbacks don't play very much is that they play the position responsible for leading the execution of that playbook on the field. That is a huge undertaking, and the training process can last months or years until the coaches feel he is ready to take on that role.

Whether you are an investor or a financial advisor helping investors, I am asking you right now to turn in your old playbook. In other words, I want you to put aside any preconceived ideas you have about how to protect and grow wealth inside an investment portfolio. By reading this book, you have been traded to a new team. This new team does not run the same, typical plays that most of the other teams run. In investor terms, that means that I will show you the weaknesses in traditional approaches to allocating and managing assets, and introduce you to a genre of investing I created. Your new "team" (investment strategy) realizes that success starts with a solid defense (i.e., a plan to limit losses when the financial markets are busy destroying value in other people's portfolios) and then tries to score enough points on offense to win games (producing solid long-term performance without a lot of flash and sizzle, and by staying out of the deep hole many investors dig for themselves).

There is an old saying in many sports that "defense wins championships." Start thinking that way, even if your investment objectives require you to achieve a fairly high long-term return. You will understand why I say this as you continue to read the book.

Your new team takes tremendous pride in not beating themselves as they have observed other teams do. I will point out common mistakes that I have seen investors make during my quarter-century in the investment industry. Your teammates are by no means mistake-free or perfectionists. They just don't tend to make big mistakes (i.e., they have a strategy to avoid major losses when markets are destroying value in their neighbors' portfolios). Big mistakes may force the team to change strategies during a game to play "catch up," and that is not desirable.

Your new team has a history of being very competitive no matter who the opponent is (I will show you how to keep your portfolio from being ruined, regardless of the market environment). They don't win every game, but they are one tough team to play against, no matter what the outcome.

While the playbook your new team uses may appear complex at times, the more you understand it, the more simple, logical, realistic, and purposeful it is to you. The strategies I will introduce you to are likely different from the traditional approaches you have seen—and in this case, different is better! But, like playing football, the exhilaration of a game plan well executed is tremendous. Welcome to your new team!

Later in this book, I'll get more specific about how to run the plays (use the strategies I created and manage today), so to speak. You may continue to follow my work at www.flexibleinvesting.net.

In Case of Fire, Use Stairs

A sign just like this was next to the hotel elevator, and I noticed it one morning while making my way down to present at an investment conference:

IN CASE
OF FIRE
USE STAIRS

At that moment, it struck me that this sign and its instructions are a beautiful metaphor for the primary message I am communicating to you: The method you take to get up to your hotel room may not be the method you take on the way down. While you don't think a fire in the hotel is likely, you do want to know what to do if one occurs. If it does, you may not be able to use the elevator. In that case, your escape route is the stairs.

What does this have to do with the approach one takes to researching and allocating investments? *Everything!* Investors have been conditioned to use the same approaches they used on the way "up" (i.e., in a strong stock market) when the market is going "down a few floors." But that may not work. There may be fires to navigate around. You may have to do what is less convenient and less comfortable—take a different approach, a different route to your goal. You may have to take the stairs instead of the elevator.

Perhaps this was so poignant to me because I was reminded of a time when I took the stairs to get down ... 97 floors. I was working near the top of the World Trade Center in 1993 when the building was bombed. This, of course, was when terrorists "missed," and limited damage and casualties resulted. For a few hours, however, we did not know what was going to happen to us. Naturally, when a true tragedy occurred in that building on September 11, 2001, and some of my former colleagues lost their lives while others escaped death by taking the stairs, it brought back memories of that day in 1993. And years later, when I noticed that sign next to the elevator in that small hotel, the investment/elevator metaphor was obvious to me. Now, I hope it is to you, too.

In this book, I plan to point out how what you can learn from the experience of the past decade, how to avoid many common investment pitfalls, and how to allocate your assets to take advantage of the realities and opportunities of today's markets. Along the way, I will help you identify, as I said in my first book, Wall Street's "bull." I intend to show you not only how to "bear it" but persevere through it. After the events of 2008, that should be a welcome sight for your eyes.

I hope this book helps you.

Rob Isbitts
Weston, Florida
June 2010

PART

I

SETTING THE STAGE TO BE REEDUCATED

CHAPTER

1

Tired . . . but Not Retired

That's what a majority of Americans predict for themselves. This book offers investors and financial advisors an investment philosophy and process to avoid that predicament. For advisors and for the do-it-yourself investor (by definition you are your own financial advisor), it allows insight into approaches and techniques that might just change the way you look at the investment markets . . . for the benefit of you and your family, for this generation and beyond.

While investors save and invest for many financial goals, in my experience the most common one is retirement. While retirement means different things to different people, the common piece of each different person's retirement definition seems to be this: the point in life at which your desired lifestyle can be paid for without your having to work. That does not necessarily mean that you don't work; many have adopted the idea of a "second career" as something they always wanted to do, but were so entrenched in their current industry that they could not afford to give up their high income level. Retirement is as much a state of mind as anything else. It's a feeling that the pressure is off, that you can comfortably afford to support yourself and those you are financially responsible for, now and in the future.

In 2006, I wrote the book *Wall Street's Bull and How to Bear It* (Isle Press, 2006). There, I reviewed many of the threats to investors and their advisors. I then suggested ways they could work together to defeat the hurdles that financial markets and financial "salespeople" put in front of those who make an earnest effort to serve their clients, so one day they can both retire. This, my second book, contains some sections of that first effort. I repeated them because today as then, they reflect my core investment philosophy.

The other reason I have duplicated parts of the first book is that so many of the warnings of that book did indeed come to pass during the awful period for investors and advisors that followed in late 2007 and 2008. My hope is that by reviewing what happened, you can learn how to be prepared for whatever comes next.

In early 2009, I read with much interest an article from Savita Iyer-Ahrestani in the April 23 online edition of *Investment Advisor* magazine. The article, "Retirement Confidence Plummets," notes that a 2009 survey from EBRI, which studies, among other things, consumer financial behavior, shows that only 20 percent of those polled are "highly confident" they'll have enough income in retirement. This is the survey's 19th year, so the results and trends over time are based in reality, in my opinion.

In this book, I will draw out a blueprint for you to take on the most pressing financial issue of our time—will investors be able to retire? To start, I'll quote from the aforementioned article, then provide my feedback.

> According to the survey, workers who say they are very confident about having enough money for a comfortable retirement this year hit the lowest level (13%) since the Retirement Confidence Survey started asking the question in 1993. Retirees also posted a new low in confidence about having a financially secure retirement: Only 20% now say they are very confident about having enough to live on comfortably in their retirement, down from 41% in 2007, the survey noted.
>
> As the general confidence level has plummeted, so too has peoples' desire to want to try and plan for the future, (Director of the study Matthew) Greenwald said. "The time when retirement planning seems toughest is when it seems harder for Americans to focus," he said.

Here is some tough love for those who may find themselves in this mind-set. Realize that if you are behind the curve on this, you don't have a choice whether to attack this problem. You have to! Sometimes investors and their advisors feel "frozen" and don't act to improve their lot when things go wrong. They become paralyzed by the seemingly numerous possible roads they can take to work out of the problem.

The shifts that have occurred in investment planning, with 401(k)s on the rocks, jobs being lost, and so on, lead you to one conclusion: you **don't** have the option to do nothing this time. Okay, tough-love section over; let's move on to another piece from the article.

> Retirement finance experts like Francis M. Kinniry Jr., a principal in Vanguard's Investment Strategy Group, believes that clients should steer the course and not give up. On the contrary, focus and clarity of thought and planning are needed more than ever, Kinniry says.

Hey, that's what I said! Yes, clarity of thought and planning. That is why many investors have sought out professional advisors (not professional investment salespeople!) for partial or total help, after doing it themselves for years, or at least since 2002, when investors last threw up their hands—after throwing up their savings—in a market whose decline was as fierce as 2008's but took three years to collapse instead of one, so it hurt one third as much (my "scientific" estimate).

> Kinniry advocates good old-fashioned investing in the stock market. "We know that the stock market has outperformed the bond market in most 10-year periods and even more so in 20-year periods," he says.

What else would you expect a partner at one of the biggest equity money managers in the world to say? Sorry, it's not that simple. "Buy and Hope" is not a strategy, especially after the emotional letdown investors have had with the markets and many of those who participated in it. I am generally bullish on the stock market over the next 20 years, but that's like saying I think the sun will come up 20 years from now. If you are right, that was to be expected. If you are wrong, no one will remember or care because they will have other things on their mind.

Also, there is bound to be a false sense of security involving bond investments, as the long-term threat of inflation from America's deficit buildup has the potential to put returns of high-quality U.S. bonds into the red, big time, for a long time, at some point.

Granted, it is not going to be easy to get people to trust in the stock market, and according to Greenwald, belief in the efficacy of equities has a taken a huge hit this year.

Call me a blind optimist (no one has called me that in many years), but when people start doubting something that has been successful many times but just lost a big battle (like the stock market did), you should reach into the closet and grab your "contrarian investor" hat. The last time I put mine on was back in 2006, when everyone said that house-flipping and real estate in general was a no-lose situation, and those who doubted that were considered out of touch. In 2007 and 2008, the pendulum swung the other way in the stock market for sure, and the crowd always overreacts at the extremes.

But Kinniry says that one of the key lessons to take away from this downturn is the importance of nuts-and-bolts investing, "the kind of stuff we learned in investing 101." With the help of an advisor—and by and large, he says, advisors have done a prudent and careful job of getting their clients to diversify among different asset classes—clients need to get a savings plan in place, and that plan should include exposure to equities.

Okay, I take back what we said earlier about our colleague from Vanguard. He made it up to us with that last statement. I think the next many years will be about two things:

1. "Renting" the stock market instead of owning it—that is, not committing to have some set percentage of money in the stock market all of the time, as static investment plans often do.
2. Applying a level of portfolio "risk management" that is not only uncommon to most investors, but foreign to some of those in the money management industry as well.

Balancing stocks with a good dose of high-grade corporate bonds or Treasuries is the best way to go. Anyone who had done this would have seen that the mix held up far better in the downturn, and that bonds are by far the best diversifier for stocks, Kinniry says.

As you will see throughout this book, I take the opposite side of this argument about **how** to diversify. Investors cannot live by stocks and bonds alone. You must add investment styles that allow you to squeeze some of the juice out of the "orange" that is the stock market, but avoid most of the rind and pits. If you still feel the urge, combine these with more traditional long-term equity approaches and use bonds only for pure preservation of capital, if you use bonds at all.

This approach makes for a more proactive response to retirement planning for all who have the courage to inquire and adopt it. I am proud to be a proponent of such an approach (and one that is increasingly being recognized as such in our industry), and I am also very pleased that my industry is getting more innovative by the day. I sense that the message is getting out that the way investors made money in the past may not be the way they will in the future. Now, a final quote from the *Investment Advisor* magazine article:

> The fact that so many people were surprised that stocks could drop so much surprises us because there have been other times when this happened, he says. But we all have very short memories and right now, with confidence at an all-time low, it is very hard to have a memory that stocks rallied off the 2002 bottom by 100%.

So true, and also a reminder that despite the cautious approach to growth investing that I espouse, you must always realize that the old rules could at some point return, for years at a time. The stock market could produce the kind of returns that get investors right back on track for retirement. As Mr. Kinniry correctly states, it has happened before.

But the question and concern this fine study and article raise is this: if the stock market fools the public again, and provides strong returns in the next decade when so many are on the sidelines, will most of them miss out, once again victims of thinking that leaves them one big step behind financial success? When the proverbial tree in the forest falls when no one is there, we must wonder, does it make a sound? Most critically for those interviewed for the EBRI survey, will it allow them to retire? If investors freeze and stay frozen, they won't hear the tree or anything else (like prudent and proactive portfolio advice) and the sounds they will fail to hear are those of the investors that shook off their fears, realized they had no choice but to fight back, and achieved a satisfactory retirement lifestyle—or better.

Over my nearly quarter of a century in the investment industry, I have developed a core investment philosophy, which I will share with you. That philosophy became an investment process, and later I developed a set of investment strategies that investors could access directly through my firm. As time went on, financial planners around the country took an interest in what I had created, and my firm and I arranged for them to access these strategies for their clients, through separately managed accounts on "wrap" platforms and through a mutual fund as well.

As markets have exploded and imploded over the years, my growing frustration with traditional investment approaches and investment products led to my developing a set of solutions that I believe strike right at the heart of what investors and financial planners truly want from their investment strategists. View this book primarily as an educational tool to help you sort through the maze of financial products and determine to what degree, if any, it fits into your portfolio (or, if you are a financial advisor, into your practice). Importantly, understand that all of this emerged from my experience as a wealth advisor, so I understand quite well what financial advisors of all types grapple with daily. My hope is that, in cases where an investor is working with a financial advisor, both can unite behind the principles and guidelines put forth in the following pages.

Bulls, Bears, and Pigs

The world of finance and investing is stereotyped in many ways. When you hear the term *Wall Street*, what do you think of? What image first comes into your mind? Is it people in slick suits walking into skyscrapers in New York City? Is it a crowd of traders huddled around a trading pit at the stock exchange? Or perhaps it's one of the stockbroker movies: *Bonfire of the Vanities*, *Trading Places*, *Wall Street*, and so on. Whatever the image is, it carries no more than a shred of truth for most individual investors. More likely, Wall Street to them is more about the reading and research they might have done for their own investments, or the investment advisor they have worked with. But all of the supposed glamour of the investment world has led, in my opinion, to a huge misconception about what it means to invest your hard-earned money and seek advice in doing so.

To start our journey to demystify some of the financial world's greatest stereotypes, and help you to separate reality from mythology, let's take a quick look at the history behind the terms *bull* and *bear,* which are commonly used in financial jargon.

A fellow named Cecil Adams wrote the following explanation on the website straightdope.com. Ironically, he wrote this back on July 11, 1986, which was right about the time I started my career in New York City:

> "Bear" is thought to have originated in a proverb that goes along the lines of, "Don't sell the bearskin before you've caught the bear." This is roughly equivalent to "Don't count your chickens before they're hatched," which is precisely what stock market bears do. Anticipating declining market prices, they sell stock they don't own yet, gambling that the price will fall by the time they actually have to buy the stock and deliver it, netting them big bucks. The term had become popular among London stock traders by the early 1700s, when the bearishly inclined were called "bearskin jobbers."
>
> The origin of "bull"—i.e., somebody who buys stock in the expectation that the price will rise—is not as clear. The term appears to have arrived on the scene a bit later than bear, and some believe it was suggested mostly by alliterative analogy to the earlier expression. The usual explanation for the choice is that bulls habitually toss their heads upward, but you could just as easily make the case that bulls get their way by bulling their way ahead—they create a stampede of optimism that prices will rise, and the inevitable result, the laws of supply and demand being what they are, is that prices do rise. However, this theory could be a load of you know what.

Investing and financial planning are not black and white. They are very gray. That is an important theme of this book. Just as achieving a balanced life is the healthiest approach, so, too, is finding the balance between potential reward and risk. The two concepts are inseparable. Trade-offs are what investing and asset allocation is all about. Otherwise, you could just load up on the investment that appears to be the best, and sit back until it pays off. People once thought of Enron that way.

Despite the importance of "gray investing," a lot of advice is given to people every day that is based on what is presented as certainty. "Invest in stocks for a decade and you'll make a lot of money. Grow your assets by 7 percent a year and you'll be able to retire at age 60." As of the end of 2008, this was nothing but a promise unfulfilled for many investors. They were understandably angry, and they should be.

I don't want to deemphasize planning. It is important. I do want to deemphasize treating the outcome of a projection as if it were reality.

Bulls and bears have ways to reach their objectives. But those who turn into investment "pigs," always trying to make a quick buck or extrapolating their recent returns into the future ("I just made 50 percent on this last year, so I'm not going to sell it—I think it will go up even more this year"), are ultimately doomed to failure.

Keep this in mind as well. The bull and bear are Wall Street's long-time symbols. The pig is also a symbol of the leanings of some investors. And as the expression goes, "Bulls make money, bears make money, pigs get slaughtered."

My work is intended to help investors get what they really want from their wealth! With that in mind, let's reexamine a year in which most investors did not get what they wanted from their wealth: 2008. In fact, by the end of February of the following year, 2009, with many stock indexes having lost over half of their value, they were probably wondering if they'd soon have much wealth left at all. And, in financial and economic environment that seemed surreal, except for the fact that it was real, they were wondering who and what they could trust.

CHAPTER 2

2008: What the Hell Happened?!

The most important lesson from the events of late 2007, all of 2008, and early 2009 was this: do not assume that just because something has never happened, it can't happen. September 11, 2001, was the ultimate example of this in the "real world," and the financial equivalent occurred later in the same decade. Lehman Brothers and Bear Stearns, gone? Citigroup and AIG sister organizations to the Department of Agriculture (i.e., all owned by the U.S. government)? Home prices plunging in value? Fannie and Freddie (ironically, the names of my wife's late grandparents who escaped Nazi Germany to start a life in the United States—but I refer to the mortgage issuers) under siege? Investment banks converting into federally chartered banks to escape collapse? The Tampa Bay Rays winning the American League pennant?

It was a year of "black swans" for sure. But the phrase "never say never" should be a part of every investor's, advisor's, and portfolio manager's DNA. As an investment strategist, I get paid to consider what our clients may not ever dream of, and to question everything, especially when an idea becomes popular or "obvious" to the mainstream.

During the 1980s and 1990s, people were lulled into a false sense of security. That led to a sense of entitlement, since in relationship to prior generations, they were denied very little. Remember "Tickle Me Elmo"? Every kid had to have one, and parents stampeded each other during the holiday season to get their hands on one. Now you can find them at garage sales. The material era is gone, but remnants still remain. That's fine, but it means that an investment strategist's job is much, much tougher. Simply educating investors is no longer the only hurdle. It's also getting them to believe that what you are telling them is valid. With the financial services industry playing the role of scapegoat more than ever before, clarity and straightforward yet innovative thinking is needed.

What was at the core of the problems that led investors to a rough 2008? In my opinion, it was not the actual market events that occurred. The events are out of our control. It was how investors and their financial advisors responded to them. Many of them didn't, believing that there was only one way to invest, and so they followed the same methods they had used for the past few decades. It is easy to understand why. Most investors and their advisors received their investment education in the 1980s–1990s, which was a historical anomaly. It was a time of nearly uninterrupted prosperity, both economically and in both the stock and bond markets. For stock market participants, 2008 broke all of the rules. In reality, the market was just reverting to its normal behavior, as reflected in much of its historical price movement and volatility since the early twentieth century. What we have now is a generation of investors who are in the early stages of a gigantic game of "investment education catch-up." This book is designed to push that educational effort further ahead, and to do so the way most systemic problems are solved—by identifying the problem and then engineering solutions. In this specific case, it is about identifying gaps in the traditional investment offering and the way portfolios are allocated. Then, we spell out how to fill those gaps. This is the essence of what this book was written to do. It is that straightforward, really.

During the summer of 2007, a short time after I published my first book, I wanted to continue to play the role I enjoy: an idea generator for and educator to investors and financial advisors. I don't refer only to investment strategy ideas, but also to supplying much-needed perspective on the events of the day that impact wealth protection and creation.

What follows is a series of articles originally presented in the *GreenThought$* newsletter I created. My hope is that you can experience some of the counsel I provided during that most stressful period, which will help you to better understand the specific investment approaches I describe later in the book. I also suspect we will have more crises of confidence in the financial markets in our lifetimes, and there are some general themes to this chapter that should help you be prepared for the next, inevitable financial nightmare.

Since we are all trying to improve ourselves every day, what we learned from how we handled 2008 will be quite valuable the next time and the time after that. I have noted each article's original *GreenThought$* publishing date. They are in chronological order, to help you experience how I instructed my audience on how to handle the financial crisis before and while it evolved.

The topics covered in this chapter may appear to be unrelated, but they all point to a central theme: in tough times, and in unprecedented times, it helps to have someone reminding you to focus, stay cool, and proceed with cautious confidence.

Where's "Voldo?"—August 1, 2007

Before the age of cable TV and the Internet, if you were in New York City on a weekday, you could always tell when the stock market was way up or way down on a particular day. You simply had to look at how big a crowd stood outside of the discount brokerage (Schwab, Fidelity) offices, watching the stock ticker, or waiting on line (this was back when online only meant standing, not surfing) to use a market monitoring machine called a "Quotron." Today, we track the markets' moves on 24-hour cable networks, the web, and our mobile phones. The information is at our fingertips. But that does not change the nature of markets, only the way we find out about what happened.

After years in which market volatility was relatively tame, the proverbial crowds may be gathering at the "virtual" office windows for the first time in a while. Market volatility is rising sharply following a long, long layoff. Like the kids game "Where's Waldo," investors may have noticed a marked reduction in volatility, and are asking, "Where's Voldo?" Well, he has returned. But is Voldo moving in or is he just in town for a short visit.

Who knows? If it's the former, it is critical to understand the implications for investors. So in this week's *GreenThought$*, we aim to help you understand what risks and opportunities a highly volatile stock market brings. First, let's explain what "volatility" is.

In layman's terms, it describes the degree to which stock prices are bobbing up and down over a period of time. To quantify this, the "volatility index," nicknamed VIX, was created in 1993 and measures volatility every minute of every day that the stock market is open.

Historically, readings have been as low as 9 during complacent periods, and have spiked as high as the 40s–60s during emotional periods such as 9/11 and the Enron fiasco. For most of the late 1990s, the 20–30 level was common.

For the past few years, the VIX has spent nearly all of its time under 20. It can be an excellent tool to gauge the potential impact of a change in market conditions.

Okay, so that's the quant-geek definition of volatility. In English, what does it mean? *Low volatility* can be interpreted as investors being complacent, not worried. *High volatility* implies an element of fear in investors' current attitudes. When volatile markets come around, it is not the actual VIX level that is most important. Understanding the way the rules of engagement for risk management and return strategies change (and they can change a lot) is the key. The difference between fearing volatile markets and capitalizing on them is, in our opinion, a key element to the long-term success of any investment strategy.

We study volatility closely and conduct research to identify investment styles that use volatility to fuel their success, not an excuse for their demise. This is one of the key facets of the strategies we have developed at Emerald, starting with our Hybrid portfolio and continuing with the creation of the rest of the Emerald Allocation Strategies (EAS) program. Voldo's here. Keep an eye on him.

"Wimpy"—September 19, 2007

Consider this, taken from www.urbandictionary.com:

> The Phrase: I'll gladly pay you Tuesday for a hamburger today.
> Definition: I'd like you to lend me some money.

Etymology is from the cartoon *Popeye*, where the character Wimpy would frequently utter this phrase. He was a glutton, and would consume burgers at a ferocious rate but could rarely pay for his habit.

The phrase implies the underlying feeling that the person will unlikely actually pay for the hamburger (or whatever) on Tuesday (or ever, for that matter).

I told my bank that I'd gladly "pay them Tuesday for a hamburger today" to buy that new sports car, but they wouldn't approve me.

Unfortunately, there have been a lot of sports cars, burgers, homes, and toys purchased with borrowed money. While there is celebration over the Federal Reserve interest rate reductions announced yesterday (a Tuesday, ironically), there is more to the story . . . but we can't write it as history yet, because it is likely bubbling up under the surface of the global economy. It's called inflation—the rate at which the prices of the things we buy go up.

Much attention is paid to the U.S. government's official releases of inflation, particularly the "core" version of the CPI (Consumer Price Index). The CPI has shown very modest increases for many years. Many market commentators will argue that "inflation is low" because the CPI is only running at a 2–3 percent rate. Without going into too much detail here in *GreenThought$*, the core CPI excludes products related to food and energy. In other words, if you didn't have to heat your home, fill your car, or eat, you would be fine. Bottom line: Don't look at the trend in CPI to figure out if inflation is an issue—but do be concerned about inflation because it is a cancer to your wealth. If you lived through the 1970s, you know what we mean.

So, where do we look for inflation indicators? We look at commodity prices—oil, gold, agriculture, etc. All have been rising for some time now. Oh, but remember, all of that oil and agriculture stuff is not "inflation" as the suit and tie crowd defines it.

One of the other areas we look at for clues as to future inflation is the bond market. No, not the overnight rates (discount and federal funds rates) controlled by the Fed, or the London Interbank Offered Rate (LIBOR) that many loans are based on. That's all short-term talk.

When it comes to long-term trends in inflation, we look at the yields of long-term bonds (10-year, 30-year maturities). They have been passive for some time, but there are issues looming like a parade of hurricanes, one behind the other: the cost of the war, the Social Security system heading toward the red (by 2017 according to one report we read recently), etc.

The question we have is: how are we going to pay for all of this? If you are the government and own the Mint, you can print more money. That pays your debts but devalues your currency (seen the

U.S. dollar's value lately?). When you hear that the Fed is "pumping liquidity into the system," there is a good reason—they are the only ones left who can.

So, the Wimpy syndrome is alive and well. Inflation is out there and it could be unavoidable, well before this decade is over. Hopefully, you can tell that we are aware of this—we have been for some time—and continue to discover strategies to combat and even exploit higher inflation if it appears in a meaningful way. In other words, we are not going to be "Wimpy" about it and stay the course. Because several Tuesdays from now, those burgers may cost a lot more.

Counting Backwards—February 1, 2008

What do these dates have in common in the history of the U.S. stock market?

1/14/08, 5/1/06, 4/9/99

Not sure? Now look at it this way:

Date	S&P 500 closing price
1/14/08	1,325
5/1/06	1,325
4/9/99	1,326

That's right. As of mid-January, the S&P 500 was essentially flat over the past 20 months, and over a period stretching back nearly 9 years! During that period since April 1999, we saw the height of the tech bubble (the market peaked about a year later in March 2000), the bursting of that bubble, 9/11, Enron/Anderson, war, and the launch of a new credit crunch (subprime mortgages, credit cards, etc.). Keep this in mind when we talk about what a secular bear market is. This is what it is.

Many investors think that a bear market is falling stock prices. That is part of the definition. To really get an appreciation for what a "secular" bear market is, you have to experience a prolonged period in which stocks are not always falling, but as the old commercial says, they've "fallen and they can't get up" to where they formerly peaked. It's ugly if you are an index investor, but it creates some very real opportunities.

As a short-term "throw-in" to this discussion, the S&P closed January down an even 6 percent. Indexes that track more aggressive equity styles fell 7 to 13 percent to start the year. Don't try to annualize those numbers, unless your cabinet is well stocked with Zantac.

The point I will make over and over to my clients and friends until I am blue in the face is this: in periods of prolonged market futility, such as what we are experiencing this decade, *investors and their advisors must recognize that their approach to portfolio management must become more flexible and adaptive.* It must be flexible to expand beyond the constraints of standard stock-bond asset allocation schemes, and it must adapt to the different set of rules that govern a secular bear market, as opposed to the secular bull market we experienced in the 1980s and 1990s. Today, simply establishing a portfolio that will largely track the market is a threat to both investors' lifestyles and advisors' businesses.

If you don't believe us, ask yourself this question: if someone showed you that based on some theory of investing from the 1980s, with academic research to back it up, the stock market always wins out over the "long run," how many years would you stick around to see if that person was right? For those that have waited patiently for 20 months, 9 years, or some time in between, the conclusion is clear—traditional strategies are not without merit, but most resort to closely tracking the market. This is **not** a complete strategy.

Compounding the problem today is that investments once considered "safe havens" now have warts. T-bill and CD yields start with a number 2 or 3, and that income is taxable for many. Insured muni bonds, once considered by many to be a "layup" for safety, are now under scrutiny as the firms that insure those bonds (MBIA, Ambac, ACA, etc.) are fighting not merely for their reputation, but their survival.

For Baby Boomers approaching retirement, seniors on a fixed income, or younger folks who are trying hard to wisely plan ahead, it's quite a frightening picture. If the market continues to drop, we'll keep tracking how far back in history we have to go to find a point in which the market is flat from that point until the current day. In other words, for how long a period have the ups and downs of the market netted us exactly one big goose egg? Much more importantly, over the next several weeks, we will track current events and provide easy-to-digest education on several analytical tools we use (and you should, too) to evaluate the past and potential success of different investment styles and money managers.

It will be interesting, and we are here to respond to your questions and concerns. Know that we are working as hard as we ever have to not only defend our portfolios in this environment, but to succeed in it, and despite it. As an example of this, during January, we increased our "dedicated short" positions in each of our three main strategies—Hybrid, Concentrated Equity, and Global Cycle. The intended effect of this is to shrink the range of possible outcomes in the portfolios, sacrificing homerun potential in exchange for a potentially higher batting average. Stay tuned.

Two Wild and Crazy Guys—August 8, 2008

The Stock Market's Split Personality and What We Are Doing About It

In our insatiable quest to rekindle pop culture memories of the 1970s and 1980s, we think back to the lovable Czech brothers (played by Dan Aykroyd and Steve Martin) from the old *Saturday Night Live* skit. The Festrunk brothers, who referred to themselves as "two wild and crazy guys," proved that when dating in America back in the disco days, a little knowledge was a dangerous thing. (For those of you too young to know what the heck we are talking about, try this link and have a laugh: www.youtube.com/watch?v= t9SaKY FR6ms&feature=related.)

The stock market has behaved like two wild and crazy guys for most of 2008. By our calculations (using data from Yahoo! Finance), in 41 percent of all trading days this year (through August 7), the S&P 500 Index closed 1 percent higher or lower than the previous day.

So, Where Are We?

To answer this question, we first have to make an assessment of the environment we are in. Whether we look at it from a fundamental or technical angle, we reach the same conclusions:

1. Stocks are in a bear market (meaning: they will be more choppy and volatile; there will be money to be made, but it won't be made as often by buy-and-hold strategies. But that doesn't mean you day-trade either!).

2. Treasury bond rates bottomed last year but the bear market that started (i.e., rising rates) has been on hold for a few months.
3. Oil and other commodities are suddenly out of favor, but only after a huge run-up. It is quite possible this is a breather, not a top in this market area.

The most common question we get these days is "what should I do in this environment?" While the specifics are up to the client and advisor working as a team, there are some broad but important guidelines we are following:

1. Be more active, as needed. "Buy and hope" is not a strategy.
2. Understand what you own—there are a lot of odd securities out there, in untested forms. No heroes, please!
3. Certain segments of the market are experiencing volatility that from a historical perspective is extremely high. Conservative portfolios should be positioned away from that as much as possible.

For our investment strategies, it has been an unusually active summer, due to the three factors cited above. To be more specific:

- We sold some positions that had appreciated nicely since we first bought them, despite a rough market environment over that time frame.
- In all three of our strategies, we made a decision to dramatically reduce our use of exchange-traded funds (ETFs) that short segments of the stock market, as well as the class of ETF known as exchange-traded notes (ETNs). These securities engage counterparties to create their structures. Call us chicken, but that counterparty risk, as with auction rate securities, collateralized debt obligations (CDOs), and the like, is something we'd rather sidestep in today's world. In place of some of those positions, we have gone back to using actively managed "bear market" stock mutual funds that we used quite a bit back in the days before short ETFs existed.
- In the Global Cycle portfolio, we sold our position in an ETF that seeks to represent the performance of a specific commodity after a very large gain over the year since we had

first purchased it. Then, in an example of how hedging transactions can function as more than a hedge, we later sold our position in a fund that shorts that same type of stock. In other words, over the different time periods we held these two positions, despite the fact that they are somewhat opposite in nature, we profited from both. It's not magic, just out-of-the-box thinking.

- In the Hybrid Strategy, we have seen in recent months how even a modest amount of exposure to commodity-related stocks can have a meaningful impact on Hybrid's volatility. We don't want that to persist, so we took steps to reduce or eliminate some positions that currently have significant exposure to energy stocks, industrial materials stocks, and, to a lesser extent, financial sector stocks.

- We are currently carrying above-average cash positions in all three strategies, though our research is uncovering some new ideas that we are preparing to introduce in the coming weeks.

"Wild and crazy" has been the story so far in 2008. But by leaning on our conservative nature, and being opportunistic when the risk/reward trade-off is favorable to us, we believe we can continue to deliver a successful long-term investment experience with only modest bumps along the way. For partiers like the Festrunk brothers, that would not be very appealing. We suspect they would be in the minority these days.

It's All About the U(-Shaped Recovery)— October 21, 2008

Here are a few more guidance points during these very confusing times for investors.

Many here in South Florida have had an affiliation with the University of Miami. Fans of the school's sports teams have a rallying cry, "it's all about the U!" We think that same idea can be applied to the eventual recovery in both the economy and global stock markets. Many will assume that stocks transition from bear markets to bull markets, rising as fast as they fell. On a very short-term basis, this can and does happen. However, like a sprinter trying to run a marathon, it runs out of gas fairly quickly.

Market strategists distinguish between "V-shaped" recoveries (in which plummeting prices are followed by rapid rises, so that a shape of a letter V is formed) and U-shaped recoveries, in which prices rattle around near the bottom (or perhaps within 20 to 30 percent of the bottom) for a while before gradually, and in give-and-take fashion, a new bull market can be established. Think in terms of years, not weeks, and your expectations will be in order. To be clear, there are still significant risks of further losses in the stock market. However, the long-term rewards of being patient and disciplined as the U eventually develops can be high.

As for the near term, we are reminded of one of our favorite lines in the history of the movies. In *Bull Durham*, Kevin Costner plays a minor league baseball catcher. After his pitcher (played by Tim Robbins) throws a few pitches that are nowhere near home plate and nearly knock the batter down, the batter looks down at Costner as if to ask what's going on. Costner replies, "Don't look at me, I don't know where it's going." *That* is today's stock market, even if you follow it closely.

That is why, while we continue to be vigilant against near-term market risk, we are now spending a lot of energy thinking about how to benefit from the ultimate recovery. Or to use yet another sports analogy, this is like a boxing match: you defend yourself first, with your gloves up, but keep looking for openings to go on the offensive. That has been our strategy for the past 12 months. While we often don't keep up with the biggest up days in the stock market, the very competitive results we've achieved over the past several months and beyond are a testament to that approach. It is okay to lose battles, just win the war—the war is the maintenance or enhancement of your lifestyle.

Why is the market so crazy on the down days lately? Our best guess: hedge funds raising cash for redemptions. Hedge fund managers are paid very well with the expectation from many investors that they will make money in any environment. Their negative returns this year have been most disappointing to their investors, many of whom have requested to get their money out. While there are various liquidity policies with hedge funds, the standard we've seen is the ability to redeem at the end of any calendar quarter, and with 45 days' notice. Redemptions in the third quarter of this year were fairly heavy, and from what we hear, they will be much larger in this fourth quarter.

It is at worst an eerie coincidence that on July 15 of this year, the S&P 500 hit what was then its intraday low for the year at 1,200. We say eerie because that is right around that 45-day notice mark before the end of the September quarter. The index then rallied about 7 percent from mid-July until the end of August, before the dramatic drop from near 1300 to the recent closing low of 900 occurred. Does that mean that the period around November 15 will have some significance? Who knows, but at a time when months' worth of "normal" market movement seem to occur within a couple of days, it makes it an interesting piece to add to our market-watching efforts.

Final thought for today: the stock market usually leads the economy. That is, stocks tend to start their move up or down before the economy heads in the same direction. We suspect this time will be no different.

We have been asked whether our market outlook is based simply on charts and analysis of market history and psychology. While we do talk about that a lot, it is more because we think it is easier for us to write about those and more enjoyable for you read about them. They are more direct answers to the kind of questions we believe investors ask themselves, as opposed to analyzing whether nonfarm payrolls data, price-to-earnings (P/E) ratios or CPI inflation translates into meaningful market ideas. Most often, those things are offered up as backward-looking explanations by market pundits, or excuses for what happened.

At the end of the day, what moves the price of an investment is what someone is willing to pay to buy it or sell it. There are certainly fundamental reasons for everything we do in our portfolios, but they have more to do with big-picture issues than the never-ending data chase conducted by the media. There are enough good economists and quant analysts that the world does not need another one. We try to add a dimension to the discussion that is often overlooked by mainstream commentators. We'll have more on this in an upcoming issue, where we'll summarize our recent portfolio changes.

Hot 'N Cold—December 9, 2008

When you have preteens in the house as I do, you can't help but stay current with what's topping the pop music charts. A recent top-10 hit by singer Katy Perry song "Hot N Cold" summarizes the stock market over the past few months. Every day at 3 PM EST, one hour before the U.S. stock market closes, it's like the "Rocky Market Picture Show"—the movie that gets played over and over to the point where you know what's going to happen, so you sing along.

The economic news is undoubtedly bad. But we must admit to an increasing feeling that much of the bad news we've seen so far is already reflected in the over 50 percent drop in the S&P 500 over the past year (from peak to trough). Actually, the stock market has long been considered a "leading indicator" of the economy. In other words, when the market started falling in October 2007, the economic news was still okay, and many "experts" were telling us that the United States and the rest of the world would see an economic pullback but avoid recession. How's that forecast working out?

As our colleague and Emerald technical analyst Michael Kahn said recently in his *Quick Takes Pro* newsletter, "We have to keep the economy and the stock market separate. Stocks already crashed ahead of the economy and they will recover ahead of the economy. And while the market heals, there will be tradable rallies and then tradable declines." . . . Dow 4,000 (i.e., a huge decline from current levels) is not in our forecast. Economic pain, unfortunately, looks to be with us for a while.

I recently looked back to a January issue of *Investment News*, one of the finest publications in the investment industry. Each year, they choose about 15 market strategists to predict stock prices and major market influences for the coming year. The S&P started the year at 1,468, and their predictions for where the S&P 500 would close in 2008 ranged from 1,810 down to 1,309. With that index closing at 876, it is fair to say that most experts were not prepared for the possibilities this year. My point is not that this is bad forecasting. It is to warn you about overreliance on forecasts. Forecasts are more a game than an element of long-term success.

Investing is not about guessing, and even when one makes a forecast, remember what I learned from staid economist Stephen Roach, then and now of Morgan Stanley, many years ago when I toiled at that firm. It goes something like "always remember to account for what will happen if your forecast is wrong." And that, very succinctly, is a powerful lesson for 2008.

So, investors should be investors, *not guessers*. Yes, it is all an "educated" guess, and you should aim to find the best-educated guessers you can, because the difference between one investment process and another is the difference between retirement and a longer working career. One of the best things you can do is avoid the "all-or-nothing" philosophies many investors are tempted to adopt in times of economic and market stress. If you approach wealth management as "it's black or it's white," or "in or out" (the Katy Perry song, remember) you are introducing an unnecessary large amount of luck into the equation.

Do you feel lucky? Unfortunately, many are stuck between "do I go to all cash?" and "I rode it down, I'll just have to ride it back up." In our opinion, both of these philosophies are extremely risky, given the short-term and long-term risk-reward analyses we are doing here at Emerald. There is an element of skill, which can be applied through thoughtful, flexible, and adaptive asset allocation (not the mass-appeal versions of allocation invented in the 1980s and still clung to today by too many investors and advisors). We'll talk more about our "twenty-first-century asset allocation" approach in many upcoming issues of *GreenThought$*. Of course, if you don't want to wait for the published segments, just call and talk to us about it.

Now, here's some excellent guidance from the aforementioned Stephen Roach, who is now chairman of Morgan Stanley-Asia. He wrote this about the U.S. economy and consumer in the *New York Times* on November 28:

> . . . This is a painful but necessary adjustment. Since the mid-1990s, vigorous growth in American consumption has consistently outstripped subpar gains in household income. This led to a steady decline in personal saving. As a share of disposable income, the personal saving rate fell from 5.7 percent in early 1995 to nearly zero from 2005 to 2007. . . .
>
> . . . Crises are the ultimate in painful learning experiences. The United States cannot afford to squander this opportunity. Runaway consumption must now give way to a renewal of saving and investment. That's the best hope for economic recovery and for America's longer-term economic prosperity. . . .

Not Suitable for All Ages?—March 17, 2009

It has been a rough couple of weeks. In fact, when you go through an episode like this one, it starts to shake your confidence in the whole system.

I'm not talking about the markets, or even the economy. The incident I refer to is my being rejected from the Career Day roster at my son's elementary school. I signed up early, and looked forward to thrilling several fourth-grade classes by explaining what investing is, and how I work as an investment strategist and mutual fund manager. As the big day approached, I received a short letter, telling me the program was full and that I would be put on the waiting list in case a firefighter, doctor, or personal trainer canceled.

It is not the school's fault that I work in the much-maligned investment management industry. Yet I can't help but wonder—has the stock market's historic drop become so severe and well known that discussing it with our future leaders is considered too upsetting or gory? The irony is remarkable. Okay, not really, but the timing was weird, don't you think?

The financial markets continued "taking investors to school," so to speak, during the first 11 weeks of the year. True to our goal of being sensitive to changes in market conditions, we have been quite active in our portfolio strategies during this time, which continues the trend that began in 2008. As our longtime investors know, we have transacted much more in our portfolios in the past year than at any time before that. The reason is simple: the times demand it. If you want to keep your wealth within spitting distance of what it once was, a more rigorous risk management process is required. We have said to many people lately that we don't enjoy being this tactical in our work, but what we like is not a priority right now. The priority is finding ways to generate competitive returns regardless of what the markets throw at us, and nimbly seizing on opportunities when they are presented.

Taken together, this barrage of activity has allowed us to position the portfolios quite differently than they were a short time ago. At the same time, we consider much of our recently added equity market exposure to be analogous to "renting" the stock market, not owning it. Exogenous news events can have an outsized impact on portfolios, and do so very quickly. Still, we are confident that we are in a position both to capitalize on a bullish market move, and to maintain all opportunities to resume a defensive stance when conditions change. We also believe our willingness to do whatever it takes to strike a balance between reward and risk while the storm blows is something our clients have come to value over the years. And that *is* suitable for all ages!

CHAPTER 3

What Have We Learned?

Now that we have relived some of the emotions of the last economic and market debacle, let's move on to what we have learned from that experience. I am proud to say that I was well in front of the curve in identifying several of the dangers lurking for investors before late 2007. Today as back then, the idea is not to predict the future, but to separate investment mythology and conventional wisdom with investment reality. I wrote quite a bit about this in my first book, *Wall Street's Bull and How to Bear It* (Isle Press, 2006). Here is an updated, post-2008 analysis of how to stay clear of trouble.

Each part of this chapter covers a different theme. What the parts have in common is that they are all lessons learned during 2008. Each covers a different segment of the investment and asset allocation approach I have espoused since the 1990s. Here is a quick summary of what we'll cover in this chapter:

- Understand that stock market history is completely different from what many investors think it is.
- "Rent" the stock market instead of owning it.
- Seek to use the stock market for what you want, instead of simply tracking its return up and down. Instead, aim to capture a majority of the market's upswings and a lesser portion of its down moves.
- Diversify in ways beyond what many "experts" consider to be diversified.
- Forget "style boxes." Stocks of different sizes and styles are often highly correlated to each other. This is especially true when stocks are falling.

- Don't invest by looking in the rearview mirror.
- Understand market history and market cycles, to better understand the potential outcomes (good and bad) that exist for you as an investor.
- Find bull markets wherever they exist (long or short).

Lessons from Stock Market History

When I first discovered the information I am about to review on stock market history, it stopped me in my tracks. Taken from the outstanding technical analysis website, www.stockcharts.com, and reprinted here with permission, we can view the entire twentieth-century price history of the Dow in 20-year segments (see Figure 3.1). I draw some important conclusions from studying over a century of stock price movements.

The period from 1980 to 2000 is generally regarded as the most profitable period in modern stock market history. But it's not the 1980s and 1990s anymore. A different approach to constructing portfolios and asset allocation is required.

From 1980 to 2000, the Dow, which is a decent proxy for the overall stock market in the United States (and, by extension, the rest of the globe) despite containing only 30 stocks, experienced a steady advance with few hiccups. There was autumn of 1987, culminating in the October 19 "crash" that left the Dow more than 30 percent off its summer high of that year. Geopolitical events such as Iraq's invasion of Kuwait (1990) and the Asian currency crisis (1998) dropped the Dow by 15 to 20 percent (using month-end values), but that was about it. The rest was prosperity: rising personal debt levels to buy video games and Tickle Me Elmo, suburbs replacing wasteland, and the rise of business TV and cable news to spread the word (good and bad news) faster than ever.

The most important point of this analysis is that the 1980–2000 period was not merely the most unrelenting rise in stock prices we've seen in the past century, it was the only one! Now, be careful how you interpret that statement. We are not saying that the stock market is a bad investment choice now that the 1990s are long gone. We actually believe the opposite—that stock market investing is a key, even vital component for the long-term growth of wealth. As I said at the start of the book, the game is the same, but the playbook needs an overhaul.

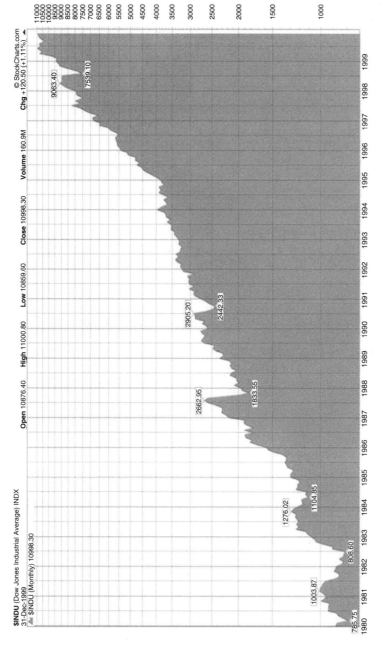

Figure 3.1   The Dow from 1980 to 2000 Was the Exception, *Not* the Rule!

Source: www.Stockcharts.com. Reprinted here with permission.

29

The stock market you think you know from investing in the bliss of the 1980s and 1990s is not the one that really exists. To put it more bluntly, expect more of what you have seen in the first decade of the twenty-first century (in which the Dow fell hard, recovered strongly for four years, and then crashed in late 2007 to early 2009, before a monstrous rally) than you remember from the 1980s and 1990s. And that is exactly where the good news starts. If you simply recognize and acknowledge that the stock market's character is not what most people think it is, you open the door to an ocean of opportunity *and* at the same time, can potentially use the stock market as a long-term risk-reduction tool!

Over the next few pages, you will see the price history of the Dow Jones Industrial Average, from 1900 to 2009. You do not need a trained chartist's eye to notice that while the 1980–2000 period was one of nearly uninterrupted advances in stock prices, the other 20-year periods showed very different patterns. We can only conclude that what we saw in the 1980s and 1990s was the exception, not the rule, for how the stock market "should" behave. This has enormous implications for you, and it is a big reason why I wrote this book.

In all other periods since 1900, stock market investing was a series of bull (up) and bear (down) markets, and sometimes over the "long term" they led to nowhere (see Figure 3.2).

Are you still thinking that maybe this is all some statistical mumbo jumbo, that it does not account for the world we live in today? One need only look at two current facts about the stock market today, in order to see that we have a point here: from 2000 to 2009, the Dow traded between about 6,400 and 14,000. My kids may tell me, "That's wacked, Dad." My response: "No, kids, that's opportunity, as long as you recognize it, and have a tested, strategic approach to take advantage of it."

Of course, they would have tuned me out after "No, kids . . . " But you don't have to. You can incorporate lower-volatility investment styles, use cash more strategically in portfolios, break your portfolios into subportfolios with varying time horizons (e.g., 3 years for this portion of the total, 5 years for that, 10 years for that, etc.) and make all of this work in your favor (see Figure 3.3).

And now, to complete this history lesson, here are price graphs for the Dow during the first three 20-year periods of the twentieth century (see Figures 3.4 through 3.6). They were not as dire and

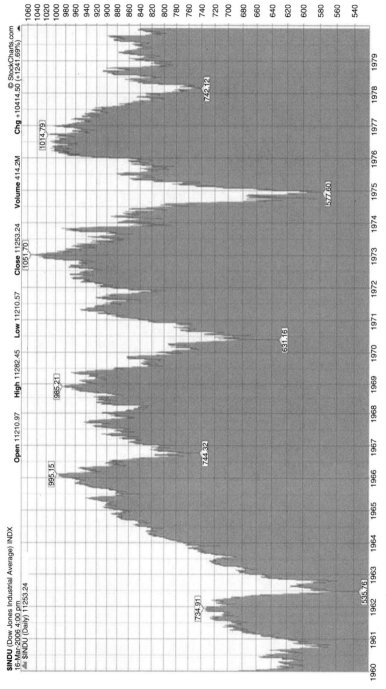

Figure 3.2   The Dow from 1960 to 1980. Sadly, This Is *also* the Stock Market!

Source: www.Stockcharts.com. Reprinted here with permission.

31

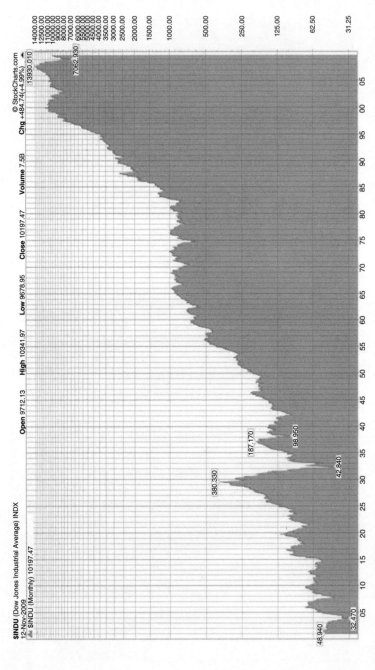

Figure 3.3   2000–2009: A Rude Awakening if You Formed Your Investment Philosophy Based on What Occurred in the 1980s and 1990s

Source: www.Stockcharts.com. Reprinted here with permission.

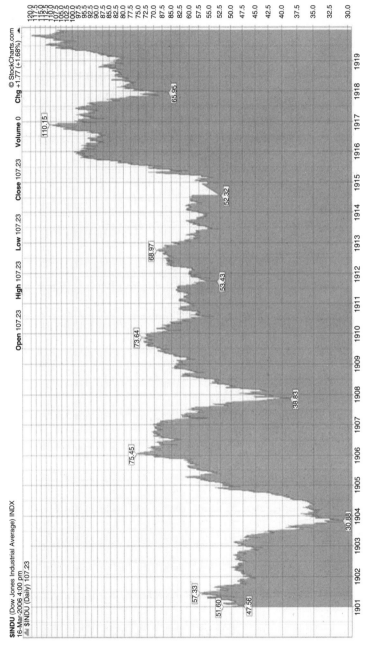

Figure 3.4 1900–1920: The Early Twentieth Century Saw Many Fits and Starts; Some Compared 2008 to the "Panic of 1907" Shown within This Graph

Source: www.Stockcharts.com. Reprinted here with permission.

33

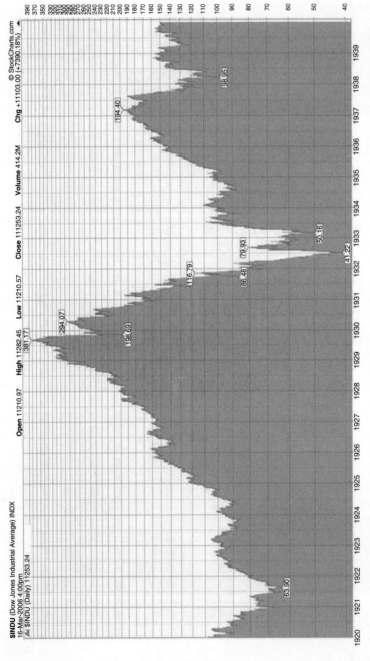

Figure 3.5 1920–1940: Between the Two World Wars, Investors Lived through the "Roaring Twenties" and the Great Depression

Source: www.Stockcharts.com. Reprinted here with permission.

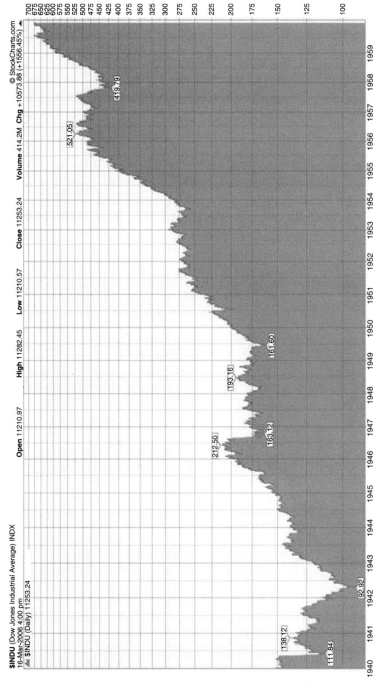

Figure 3.6 1940–1960: The Runner-up—the 1980s–1990s Bull Market, but with Plenty of Anguish Along the Way

Source: www.Stockcharts.com. Reprinted here with permission.

enduring as the 1960–1980 period, but they in no way resemble the 1980–2000 period. We need to face the fact that stock market history is entirely different from what the media and the big Wall Street firms want you to believe. The latter, despite their elegant TV commercials to the contrary, still operate largely in a commission-oriented, product-pushing, firm first–client second environment. Independent advisors, however, appear to have received the message loud and clear. From my experience, they have been much more receptive to the idea that the stock market is to be navigated, instead of implicitly trusted. That kind of innate skepticism is what you want from someone you consult to advise you on your hard-earned wealth!

I've never quoted and paraphrased Rudyard Kipling before (though I have read Kiplinger's—does that count?), but here goes:

> If you can keep your head when all about you
> Are losing theirs . . .
> If you can trust yourself when all men doubt you,
> But make allowance for their doubting too . . .
> . . . Yours is the Earth and everything that's in it,
> And—which is more—you'll be a Man, my son!

My experience has taught me that basic human behavior in the stock market does not change significantly from generation to generation. Panic and euphoria have been and always will be the "mainstream" thinking on Wall Street.

We just analyzed the U.S. stock market from 1900 to 2008. It is most ironic that Kipling's poem "If" is still as important today as it was when he wrote it—in 1895, five years before this market history review started. That "herd mentality" you read about in the *Wall Street Journal* or *Money* magazine is a herd that keeps reproducing, creating new generations of lemmings. Don't be one of them.

"Renting" the Stock Market—the Ballad of Babe and Yogi

Consider the tale of two investors, Babe and Yogi. Lest you think that those references are to the baseball legends Ruth and Berra, I am not using a baseball analogy.

Babe is an investor who trusts the stock market to eventually come through for him. He would consider himself a generally "bullish" investor (Babe was the name of Paul Bunyan's blue ox, and a bull and an ox are both bovines). Thus, Babe keeps his portfolio invested in index mutual funds and exchange-traded funds (ETFs), with the objective of matching the return of the stock market in good times and bad. After all, he says, "The market will always bail me out."

Yogi is an animated fellow (like Jellystone Park's most famous resident). Yet he does not implicitly trust the stock market, and after what he's seen since last summer, his conviction is stronger than ever. He does not dislike equity investing; in fact, it is the core of his portfolio. He likes the fact that he has daily liquidity in his investments, as equity mutual funds and ETFs provide. However, he is neither a day-trader nor a buy-and-hold index investor. He is somewhere in between, and over the years has sought out ways to use the stock market for what he wants out of it—a liquid, transparent way to grow his wealth over time.

Yogi is a "bearish" investor, but his friends tell him he's "smarter than the average bear" in one important respect (see Figure 3.7). He does not think the stock market will always go down, but he leaves room in his portfolio approach so that he can be very bearish when he wants to, and decidedly bullish when he concludes that the long-term outlook for stocks is positive. You might say he is bullish on the ability for markets to recover from anything, but bearish on the philosophy of always staying fully invested in

Babe
- Generally "Bullish"
- "Investing in stocks is patriotic"
- Buy-and-Hold index and big-name mutual funds
- "In the long run, the market will bail me out"
- Achieves rock-star status in bull markets

Yogi
- "Bearish" by nature (literally)
- "Flexible and Opportunistic"
- "Buy and Rent"— depends on situation
- "Market = an orange — squeeze the juice"
- Balances risk and reward ALWAYS

Figure 3.7   Meet Babe and Yogi

stocks. He refers to this as "renting the stock market" instead of owning it.

He believes that by incorporating hedging techniques in his portfolio (but using mutual funds and ETFs, thereby avoiding individual stock risk and complex investment structures like limited partnerships), and raising some cash at times when he feels the market's risk/reward is not in his favor, he can squeeze out market-beating returns over time. Of much greater importance, Yogi feels that his approach to portfolio management gives him a higher likelihood of retiring to a lifestyle of his choosing, rather than one that is dictated by how the stock market happened to do during the period he was invested. He has seen how retirees have lost so much in the past year, particularly those who had built enough wealth to retire in the style they dreamed of, only to see it taken away in a few months.

Yogi knows that his portfolio will often not be as "sexy" as Babe's, as it will likely not jump the way Babe's does when the market is bopping. He does feel that in the best of times, he will get his fair share of the ups, and that playing good defense in tough times is far more important in increasing his chances of reaching his eventual goals. He figures if he can get roughly two thirds or more of the stock market's gains over extended bull cycles, and keep losses to about one third or less of the market's decline in extended down cycles, that will be a winning combination.

Both Yogi and Babe have no idea when that lost wealth from 2008 will eventually be recovered, or even if it will be, but they ponder that from very different perspectives. For illustrative purposes only, here's why (using hypothetical figures and returns for these hypothetical investors):

Date	Babe's Portfolio	Yogi's Portfolio
January 2008	$100	$100

Babe and Yogi both had $100 when the frightening investment year of 2008 began. At year-end, here's where they stood:

Date	Babe's Portfolio	Yogi's Portfolio
December 2008	$60	$85

The market continued to fall in early 2009, leaving the two investors here:

Date	Babe's Portfolio	Yogi's Portfolio
March 2009	$45	$80

The market rallies in March and into early April, and Babe is feeling very good again. His portfolio is up over 20 percent in just five weeks! Yogi made money, too, but at a far lower rate, about 12 percent. His portfolio, as it typically does, trails the market by a wide margin in these short, sharp rallies, though it tends to grab a much bigger share of the pie during more extended up moves. Here's where they stand now:

Date	Babe's Portfolio	Yogi's Portfolio
April 2009	$55	$90

Babe is celebrating what he feels is the beginning of much better things in his portfolio. Then he stops in for a latte and sees his buddy Yogi. Babe, who tends to think about his portfolio in dollars, not percentages, brags about the $10 he's made in just over a month. Yogi congratulates him, and then explains that he also made $10 during that time. Babe asks Yogi, "Did you finally see it my way and start investing in the market instead of that hedged growth thing you do?" Yogi thinks about it for a minute and states the conclusion and lesson from this story: "Babe, old pal, I had $80 when the market started coming back, so I made $10 in real money by only making 12 percent. Your portfolio had dropped so far in the tough times that you needed nearly more than a 20 percent gain to make the same $10 I just did. It seems like your money has to work a lot harder than mine every time the market falls."

Babe thinks about it and then realizes that it might be time to consider more seriously whether he should replace his method with Yogi's, or at least make some room for it alongside his traditional investing method. Babe and Yogi agree that given the goings-on in the world, this won't be the last time the market swings up and down like this. Thinking about this makes Babe turn, well, blue. He and Yogi finish their lattes and Babe feels a lot better (and not because of the caffeine). He realizes that while his way worked for a long time, he now needs to consider the simple math behind gaining and losing in the stock market. Going forward, he wants to avoid making any more "Boo-Boos." He commits to figuring out how "renting the stock market" can work in his favor, too.

The 60/40 Approach to Investing—My Version

In difficult markets, we are inundated with comparisons to ugly eras of the past. One that I have discussed many times internally and with our clients is the period from 1966 to 1982. Some of today's senior citizens may remember this period as investors and the challenging period it was for making money. Others will remember it as a time of war, volatile gas prices, and significant social changes, all of which have reappeared in the current decade. And, let's face it— some people who lived through the late 1960s and early 1970s may not remember it at all—if you know what we mean.

1966 to 1982 was a period in which stock prices rose and fell every few years, but did not make sustainable progress. As we have pointed out in *GreenThought$*, and on conference calls with clients and financial advisors recently, there have been many periods in market history in which this market stagnation existed. In fact, according to the web service Chart of the Day, "since 1900, the Dow has undergone a major correction 26 times or one major correction every 4.2 years." In other words, long-term investors should get used to them.

This may sound dire, but, in fact, what we are pointing out is the urgent need for investors to have a strategy to weather any market condition. That is not the same as making money in every market cycle, but it does mean that we have to have a strategic discipline that adapts to ever-changing circumstances. Unfortunately, most investment approaches do not do that, and it causes emotions to run higher than they should. This, in turn, leads to many terrible, panicked decisions by investors.

With that as a backdrop, let's consider what I call the "60/40 approach" to portfolio management. Wall Street veterans may think we are talking about the standard advice of putting 60 percent of your money in stocks and 40 percent in bonds to create a "balanced" portfolio. Given the historically low (pathetic?) yields on high-quality bonds, and the record high stock market volatility, such standard advice is, in our opinion, like offering someone a drink at a bar, but not telling them it is actually a Molotov cocktail!

Let us explain what 60/40 means to us, and show you how applying it might just be the key to surviving the economic and market wars of the coming years. We'll use the Dow Jones Stock Index price history from the difficult 1966–1982 period to tell the story.

During that 16-year period, the Dow saw the following changes. These changes lasted between one and four years each:

- DOWN 25 percent, then UP 32 percent
- DOWN 36 percent, then UP 67 percent
- DOWN 45 percent, then UP 76 percent
- DOWN 27 percent, then UP 22 percent
- DOWN 16 percent, then UP 35 percent
- DOWN 24 percent

So, for every $100 you started with in 1966, you had $78 in your pocket by 1982. That does not include the effects of rapid inflation during the period. Government bonds were yielding double digits during part of this time, but they were not very attractive given constantly rising consumer prices. Today, we have the threat of inflation but the cushion of big yields is not there. Trouble? Enter the 60/40 strategy.

The concept is simple to understand. It has two parts:

1. During each stock market up-cycle (measured in multiyear peaks and troughs, not in days/weeks/months), strive to earn at least 60 percent of the market's move. That is, for every 10 percent move up in the market, make at least 6 percent in your portfolio.
2. During each stock market down-cycle, strive to limit losses to 40 percent of the market's decline. So, for each market decline of 10 percent, limit losses to 4 percent in your portfolio.

Naturally, these are target minimums, but the 60/40 idea reminds investors and their portfolio managers not to get greedy in good times, and to *manage risk effectively in down times.*

No, we don't know exactly when cycles start and end. It's kind of like the National Bureau of Economic Research (NBER), the agency that is charged with determining when recessions begin. They officially named the most recent one a full year after it started, but anyone with their head in the game could confirm that fact several months before NBER called it.

It's the same with the stock market, which goes through up and down cycles as well as what we refer to as "transition" cycles. Our best guess at Emerald is that we are in a transition cycle now, from a down market to an up market. But that does not mean we "back up the truck" to buy equity mutual funds like it's the roaring 1990s. It is more of an awareness exercise. Only by closely studying the progress of these cycles as they develop do we gather enough confidence to eventually get more bullish in our portfolios. We are thankful to our technical analyst, Michael Kahn, for helping us in the judgment of this.

So, how did 60/40 work from 1966 to 1982? Using the same format as we did for the Dow Jones:

- DOWN 10 percent, then UP 19 percent
- DOWN 14 percent, then UP 40 percent
- DOWN 18 percent, then UP 45 percent
- DOWN 11 percent, then UP 13 percent
- DOWN 7 percent, then UP 21 percent
- DOWN 10 percent

Bottom line: For a growth investor, the 60/40 returns, if achieved, would have kept emotions at bay and allowed for strong benefits in up markets. In fact, while the Dow itself turned $100 into $78 over the period we presented here, the 60/40 approach allowed you to grow that $100 to $159. That is not a sensational annualized return, but it is more than double what your portfolio amounted to with a stock index strategy. In other words, aggressive investing did not help, but a process that included good risk management and opportunistic investing did.

This lesson is certainly not limited to situations in the distant past. A simple look at the 2008–2009 period for the S&P 500 shows the basic weakness of the "high market correlation is good" argument. As Figure 3.8 shows, a major decline in your portfolio needs more than a single strong recovery to make up for it. And the longer it takes just to get back to even, the longer it will take you to actually profit from your investment experience. Life is short; losing a lot of time waiting just to recover what you have lost is more difficult

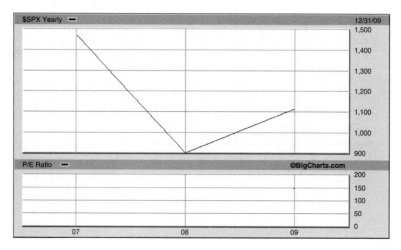

Figure 3.8   Even Strong Recoveries (2009) Look Weak after Big Declines (2008)

than many investors imagined—but after 2008 and 2009, they now know better.

What is clear is this: your odds of success, emotionally and financially, can be greatly improved by employing a strategic approach that "plays great defense and has enough offense to win."

There Must Be 50 Ways to Invest Your Assets

When Paul Simon composed the 1975 song "50 Ways to Leave Your Lover," he was writing about his ex-wife, not his investment portfolio. Given the cross-currents in the world financial markets, however, we thought it was a good time to remind you of just how much investment flexibility exists for investors and their advisors today.

As a money manager, I live by two key themes:

1. **Be flexible:** When making money is easy for the pro or amateur investor, you don't need much flexibility, just a set of darts and today's newspaper, opened to the mutual fund or stock section (if your local paper still carries this). Flexibility to invest in a wide variety of market segments and themes, and having the ability to make the right long-term choices among those themes, is the key to the work of any asset allocator. We have found it is not only the skill of the manager that

gives you potential for success, but the size of the toolbox at their disposal. More tools allow you to create more scenarios to profit from, whether your time horizon is a few years or a generation.

2. **Be adaptive:** Market environments change, and sometimes this occurs suddenly. In secular bear markets such as we are experiencing now in global equities, these changes can be rapid. That in itself does not necessarily signal you to adapt to each change. However, if market cycles in a particular area now complete themselves in a fraction of the time they did during the bull markets of the 1980s and 1990s, it calls for an adjustment in the approach you take to your own buy-sell behavior. "Buy and hold" can become "buy and hope" if this is not recognized. That does not mean you go from being a long-term investor to trading your portfolio; it simply means that subtle adjustments in your expectations for an investment are a necessary part of long-term success.

So, with a nod to Paul Simon, we present a list we compiled of "50 Ways to Invest Your Assets." They are in no particular order, and by no means is this an exhaustive list. We have focused on what is available in daily-liquid public securities markets (stocks, mutual funds, ETFs). Some of the members of the list may surprise you—the world is gradually recognizing that there is more to portfolio management than traditional stock-bond approaches, and you don't need to be a hedge fund manager to access them. See how many you have invested in and what you may be missing out on as time goes on. If you need an explanation of any of them, just email us and we'll fill you in.

Be flexible, be adaptive. There must be 50 ways (at least!) to do it (see Figure 3.9).

We'll talk about "flexible and adaptive" investing throughout this book. In fact, if you remember just one thing from all of this material, let it be that phrase. But, hopefully, you will remember more than that.

Style Boxes: Out of Style?

Morningstar, the database and securities analysis company, is known for, among other things, the "style box." This grid contains nine

Figure 3.9 50 Ways to Invest Your Assets

boxes, and each box represents the type of investment (growth, value, or core—mix of growth and value) and the size of the companies involved (large, medium, or small cap). The style box spawned an entire segment of the investment industry. It literally took the concept of asset allocation and put it on the map. Morningstar even supplied the map.

Style-box investing was all the rage in the investment advisory profession during the 1990s. In fact, if you look at how mutual funds and managed accounts are created today, a lot of it goes back to the producer's desire to build a product to fit an area of the style box. It is common to see a company with a single mutual fund, which did not have a clear style bias, renamed, say, the "Large Core Portfolio." The management company would then introduce a Large-Cap Growth Portfolio and a Large-Cap Value Portfolio. Later on, they would build or acquire a small-cap fund, and perhaps a mid-cap, too. They'd keep going until they were confident that their sales force could now go out and market to advisors, armed with their own brand of box-filling products.

I think that this is very 1990s thinking, and it is potentially detrimental to you as an investor. The reason is simple: style-box investing does not reduce your risk as much as you think it does!

Unwrapping the Box

One money management firm we know touts their firm's flexibility in being able to invest in any stock style whenever they want. At the same time, they run a fairly concentrated portfolio. They refer to their philosophy as "unwrapping the box," which is clearly aimed at refuting the style-box mentality in today's postbubble environment. I'm right there with them. Investing for the next generation, in my opinion, is more about maintaining the highest possible degree of flexibility, not clinging to a rigid, boxy style of portfolio construction. I don't see anything in the latter approach (style box) that cannot be accomplished by the former (flexible). I think that the investment industry is slowly starting to pick up on this.

Individual investors who do their homework will pick up on this sea change over time. I am more concerned about financial advisors, since this style-box mentality is so ingrained in what is pitched to them, over and over again. It's comforting to be with the herd— until it runs off and leaves you alone, in the dust.

If advisors and their firms do not take a good look at the changing face of asset allocation and continue to live in the 1990s, they risk going the way of the bulky, three-pound mobile phones we used early in that decade. I think my little girl, Morgan, used to play with an old one. And when she was done pretending to talk on it for a few seconds, she would throw it on the floor and go on to something else. I don't want to be that mobile phone, and neither do you!

In the spirit of the widely watched CNBC host Larry Kudlow, I believe that the "best path to prosperity" is a portfolio management strategy that is **flexible** enough to navigate a wide variety of market conditions, and has the ability to be **adaptive** to major changes in market conditions over time. That path also includes something akin to the 60/40 approach I described earlier.

The strategies I created developed out of a concern we had years ago that there are gaps in the traditional investment offerings that needed to be filled and that hedge funds are not for everyone, even if you can afford them. That's my story. I am definitely sticking to it.

"Rearview Mirror" Investing

This is one of the most blatant violations of the rules investors should beware of: for some reason, many people get into the habit of wanting to buy today what they wished they could have owned in the past.

Maybe there should be a sticker on lists of recent top-performing mutual funds: "Warning: you may be too late to enjoy any of this!" While recent performance may be attractive, the numbers alone do not tell the whole story. What drove the performance? Was it an overall tendency in the market, an indication of the success of the investing methodology of the fund, or the result of random events and blind luck? The most important question regarding performance is: Are the conditions that led to such performance likely to continue? Is performance sustainable? This is where detailed and professional analysis comes into play.

The other issue regarding investing through the rearview mirror is one that made headlines in late 2008. Bernard Madoff, revered for decades as a leader on Wall Street by peers and regulators alike, turned out to have everyone fooled. In particular, he made fools out of the Securities and Exchange Commission, and brought to light some serious internal problems at that industry watchdog.

While the Madoff event and others like it have changed the nature of securities regulation for the rest of our lives, there is hopefully some good that will come out of the greatest financial disaster of our lives. After the many disheartening events of 2008, all investors should make investment education a high priority. This not only means they should gain a proper understanding of the basics of securities markets and how they work. It also should make them strive for a deeper understanding of not only what they are invested in, but how their results should be interpreted. In the Madoff situation, it appears the only way one could truly have uncovered the fact that all investment statements and the performance track record were fake is to have gained access to the private room on the 17th floor of the so-called Lipstick Building in New York City, where Madoff pumped out the forged documents.

For the purposes of this book, let's take a giant leap of faith and conclude that nothing of that level of fraudulent activity will occur again in our lifetimes. We then drop down to the next level of concern: if you rely on past performance in part as a determinant of your investment decision making, how do you increase the chances that the performance numbers you are reviewing are indeed real? That is, are they not only accurate but complete, and are they a true representation of what you are investing in?

It is one thing to have a set of strategies that can produce the desired results for an investor. It is another to have confidence that the past performance results you are shown are reliable. Of course, this is particularly important when an investor is considering a strategy but has not invested money yet. Like it or not, we are in an era where so much investment "performance" is actually simulated or back-tested data and not based on actual accounts invested. It has gone on this way for many years, and while there are signs that regulators are starting to seriously toughen up in this area, nothing happens that quickly in the investment management business.

For investment firms that cater to institutional clients, past performance data is often run through the most stringent performance audit test in our business, the Global Investment Performance Standards (GIPS). In 2009, I asked Donna Naitove, an experienced chief compliance officer, to comment on the significance of the GIPS as a protective feature for prospective institutional investors. Here is what she said:

> The Global Investment Performance Standards were created so that investment management firms had a set of universally accepted ethical guidelines to compute and present investment performance. Adherence to these standards provides a high level of credibility to the calculation and presentation of investment performance history. Emerald has committed to presenting their performance according to GIPS, and devotes considerable resources to maintain its claim of GIPS compliance. Emerald has also employed a third-party verification service to verify the firm's compliance with the standards and to examine its marketed composites' performance.

Finding Bull Markets Wherever They Exist

Remember the 50 ways to invest your money that I listed for you a few pages ago? Now, look at that list again. There is a good chance—no, a *great* chance—that in any market and economic environment, at least some of these will produce positive returns. While that may not be enough for you to make money when the market is down 20 percent, it may very well stave off lifestyle-changing drops in your wealth. And that, after all, is what bear market management is all about.

Here are some brief examples of where you might start your search for investment styles and strategies that could yield satisfactory results, if you find yourself in a particular market or economic condition. By no means is this an exhaustive list. Also, note that not every situation plays out exactly the way it has in the past. One of the most difficult parts of 2008 as a money manager was the fact that some relationships that occurred in the past between markets did not hold up. That is when the value of an adaptive approach to portfolio management is so valuable.

With that said, Table 3.1 shows a primer on figuring out "where the bulls are."

The point of these few examples is to reassure you that in any market environment, there are ways to seek profits. That does not mean that your entire portfolio will make money. Remember, the goal should not be to make money every day, every week, every month, or even every year. Why not? Because that will cause you to make decisions that are too far to the bullish or bearish side of the market. If you are right, you feel like a star. If you are wrong, you get what billionaire and onetime U.S. presidential candidate Ross Perot called "that giant sucking sound." He was referring to the potential loss of U.S. jobs to Mexico from the North American Free Trade Agreement (NAFTA) bill. I am talking about the dollars coming out of your portfolio because you made a big bet instead of considering, analyzing, and truly managing the balance of risk and reward in your portfolio.

Also note that the biggest "bull markets" in a particular market environment could be strategies that include shorting stocks or bonds. When I speak to groups, I often ask the question, "Where were the bull markets in 2008?" Occasionally, someone will shout out "U.S. Treasury Bonds," as they appreciated when investors

Table 3.1   Likely Bull Markets in Differing Economic/Market Situations

Economic/Market Situation	Where the Bulls Are
Early stage of economic recovery	Contrarian value
	Long-short equity
	Global infrastructure
	High-yield bonds
	Convertible securities
	High return-on-equity (ROE) growth stocks
Strong/sustainable global economic growth	Emerging-market equity
	Frontier markets U.S. small-/mid-cap equity
High-fear investor environment	Market-neutral equity
	Arbitrage strategies
	Hedged equity strategies
	Tactical investing
	Dedicated short equity
High inflation expectations	Inverse fixed income
	Gold
	Currency strategies
	Treasury inflation-protected securities (TIPS)

hoarded Treasury securities when it appeared for a while that nothing else was safe. That is correct, though I don't think forecasting panic-buying scenarios can be too big a part of one's analysis.

I then explain that 2008's biggest bull markets were in shorting stocks—many types of stocks, in fact. Think of it this way: if you had even a modest portion of your portfolio in mutual funds or ETFs that rise when some part of the stock market falls, you would add some positive return to your overall portfolio from that segment of it. This would likely not be sufficient to make your entire portfolio profitable in a year like 2008. However, you would have achieved a major victory in two ways: You had a portion of your portfolio that made money when gains were very hard to come by. Also, by producing gains with that portion of your capital, less of your total capital was subject to the horror that was a rapidly declining stock market in 2008.

As a result, you likely have kept your total assets at a high enough level to position yourself confidently for the next eventual up market cycle. Remember, successful growth of one's portfolio can be achieved many ways. In my strong opinion, the best way to do it is by capturing your fair share of the ups (this does not mean taking on the risk of getting all of the ups), while defending yourself so that you capture only a portion of the downs.

PART II

GETTING OLD IDEAS OUT OF YOUR HEAD

4

Identifying the Issues and the Enemy

Now that we've discussed what happened in 2008 and what we learned from it, let's move on to the environment and challenges faced by investors today. Unfortunately, many of them are the same ones I was writing about many years ago. This is why a massive reeducation process for investors is required, and why this book hopefully will be part of the spark that allows that reeducation to occur. It will be a long battle, perhaps a generation in length, before it is commonly practiced. But it will be worth it.

If the decades of the 1980s and 1990s were about investing becoming more of a mainstream activity, the next decade may be about adjusting to an environment in which the mainstream was taken advantage of. From Wall Street scandals to new investment vehicles, a lot has changed, and it changed quickly. If you are devoted to the idea of maintaining an investment plan for the long run, you have two choices. You can educate yourself about what is real and what is a myth at investment firms and within investment products. Or you can throw caution to the wind and hope you are placed in appropriate investments by qualified advisors, or determine how to choose them on your own.

What Makes Today Different from the 1980s and 1990s?

I am proud to say that I wrote much of this section to my clients back before most of it was portfolio-saving information for investors.

Fortunately, I put these ideas to good use during the raucous period that followed later that decade. Investing is a very different venture today than it was in the 1980s and 1990s. That is important because it seems to me that the majority of investors and financial advisors learned about investing during those two decades. We tend to believe our own experience about things instead of looking at what happened before we were invested in a style or strategy. For instance, if you were invested in a mutual fund that had done really well for many years before you bought it, but had slipped up a bit since you bought it, what would you think of that fund? I have seen many situations where an investor would look at that fund and consider it a failure. They were only considering their own experience with it, not looking at the entire track record or the market environment in which they owned the fund.

Similarly, if you learned the ins and outs of investing in the 1980s and 1990s, you learned that markets go up, and when they decline, it's not for long and the drops are minimal. That was the experience of the late twentieth century. Thus, when a decade like 2000–2009 occurs, and markets behave differently, there is a tendency to cling to the approach that worked in the two decades prior. *That*, in my opinion, is what cost investors more money than anything else. The stock market fell for many reasons, and also had some very good times in between the drops. However, it was not the volatile markets that tripped up investors and their advisors. It was their failure to adapt to the realities of the current environment. On the next few pages is my short list of reasons why, and explanations. And the fact is that the first decade of the twenty-first century was a lot like most of the twentieth century. The period from 1980 to 2000 was the exception, not the rule! Thus, a massive reeducation effort is needed, so that there is a keen awareness about all the possible outcomes for you when you invest in the public securities markets.

The concept of twenty-first-century asset allocation versus what became the standard approach in the 1980s and 1990s starts with an understanding of the following concepts:

- *Absolute vs. relative return.* In the bull market decades, investors became index trackers. If they used an active money manager instead of an index fund, that manager was considered a failure if they did not consistently exceed the return of the relevant index. People who considered a return of 25 percent from an active manager when the index made 30 percent a "failure" were missing an important point: 25 percent return is a lot of money! Yet the investor was not focused on the "absolute return" of 25 percent, but rather on that figure's shortfall "relative to" the index. This has also led to many misconceptions about indexing as a strategy. To summarize, people love indexes in up markets, but when they realize that in down markets, they lose whatever that index does, the love affair ends faster than a Pamela Anderson marriage.

Investors are quickly getting familiar with the pursuit of absolute return on a consistent basis. That is, they are far more likely today than before to say something like "I just want to make 5 to 8 percent each year." If they are rational, they will realize that this is not something that can easily be achieved every year, unless they can get that return on high-quality bonds. But that is more of a gamble than at any time in our investment lifetimes, given the credit shock of 2007–2008, where institutions failed (or were rescued) and consumers' debt-heavy habits came back to bite them in a nasty way. More on that in a moment. With the steady, predictable results of bond investments now less certain, you can't just "lock in" a 6 percent return and feel like you are in the clear for a while.

This situation caused financial advisors and investors to start searching for alternate routes toward consistent returns. I am happy to say that my team and I were way out in front of this concept, so we were happily waiting when it suddenly became the "in" thing to do. We think it could be a generation before people will start to forget what they have been through, and that means that relative return investing will now share the stage with the pursuit of absolute returns.

Keep in mind that nothing described in these pages will guarantee a return in a particular range. Anyone who says they can do that is lying, as we found out when Ponzi schemes blew up all over the world. We will focus not on perfection, but on growing capital in as straight a path as possible, but knowing full well that down years and certainly down months and quarters are very much a part of the process.

- *Awareness of secular markets.* The events of 2008 caused a greater awareness of everything financial. But awareness is not enough. As noted earlier in this chapter, secular market periods, whether bull or bear, must be recognized and adapted to. Since these periods evolve over some time, this is not a judgment that needs to be made with urgency. However, you can't just blindly set an investment strategy without having some sense of the secular environment and how it will affect that strategy. What I have tried to build over the years is an investment process that allows portfolios to be constructed very differently at one end of the spectrum (secular bear markets) than at the other extreme (secular bull markets), with many gradients in between.

As we discussed in previous chapters, a bear market is an extended period of time during which stock prices are roughly flat. That's right: not down, flat. Secular bull and bear markets have lasted between 8 and 20 years, and the average return across the length of a secular bear is slightly above to slightly below zero.

Wait a minute! Aren't secular bears huge, nasty declines? Yes, partly. Think of it this way: Suppose the S&P 500 index lost about 45 percent in two and a half years (as it did during 2000 to 2002). Using some basic math, that means it will take a 90 percent rise to return to the old highs. If that moves takes 10 years, we will have had a 12-year period with zero return. That's a secular bear market.

Bear market recoveries, however, are more often gradual than quick and exciting. The whiplash effect that was the stock market rally beginning in March 2009 saw the S&P 500 gain 20 percent in about two weeks, on the way to a powerful, head-scratching gain of over 60 percent by the time the year had ended.

The question in evaluating any recovery is its sustainability. In other words, is the market surge simply another leg in a long, choppy market like we saw earlier in the historical charts of 1960 to 1980? Let's say that after losing 30 percent from the market's high point in a year, it took you 5 years to get back to the old highs, you'd average over 7 percent a year and finally get back to where you started 6 years before. Try explaining to your family that your retirement plan was based on an assumption that stocks always go up in the "long run" and that the plan you put in place with those index funds

12 years ago netted you about zip in return. I guess you'll need another phase on that retirement plan. With the rising concerns that employees of large corporations have about the future availability of their pension plans, avoiding the potential trap of failing to adjust to a secular bear market is, in my opinion, the greatest challenge faced by Baby Boomers, who will hit retirement age in large numbers over the next three decades.

Secular bear markets call for very different investor behavior. In fact, I think that given the four statements above, it is essential to change the way we have been taught to think by the media, by brokerage firms, and even by many advisors.

- *Inflation/rising interest rates.* Interest rates generally fell from the early 1980s through the first decade of the twenty-first century. As a result, investments in high-quality bonds posted their best returns in history. Even if rates continue to fall over the next decade, they are now starting from a much lower rate level. That means that the gains many have experienced in bond funds that invest in U.S. Treasuries, high-grade municipals, and high-grade corporate bonds that many have seen as a birthright for over nearly three decades will not be matched. It changes the whole way we look at bond investing. So the key question to ask is: Will inflation become a threat to wealth again? And if it does, will you know what to do about it?

Given the aforementioned problems that occurred in the credit markets in 2007 and 2008, what we are left with is the end of the era when you could own many types of bonds (municipal, corporate) without fear. In its place, we have the start of another era: the slow, painful process known as "deleveraging." As consumers and governments around the globe relearn how to act prudently with regard to money, very little is assured in the bond market. It is true that U.S. Treasuries are still one of the most reliable creditors out there, so if you buy their bonds, fear that you will not be repaid is still pretty farfetched, I think. However, the concern you should have even with Treasury securities is that interest rates will rise furiously over the next decade, leaving your existing bonds with very uncompetitive yields.

Remember when inflation rates were over 15 percent? I don't. I was in grade school, and, while I started my curiosity of the financial markets at a fairly young age, I was not infatuated with the study of markets just yet (still wanted to be a baseball player or a fireman or something). But it's not important whether you were old enough to remember the last period of hyperinflation in the United States. What is important is that you are prepared in case an environment such as that occurs again—and most likely it will.

Why am I so confident about this? Because the economy, like human behavior and much of life in general, is cyclical. What was gone forever somehow comes back. Bell-bottoms? Back. Coca-Cola in glass bottles? Back. Inflation so high it impacts your daily life and every financial decision you make? Well, it may come back. From the early 1980s through the beginning of the twenty-first century, seeing your "cost of living" for most basic items increase by 2, 3, or maybe 4 percent was typical. Maybe it will be for a long time. But history is against us on this one.

I am not trying to make a short-term prediction here. This book is not about that. I'm just trying to plant a seed in your mind that your portfolio's life is *very* different in a high-inflation environment. Want a quick example? Let's say you and your advisor have great confidence in the plan you crafted, with an 8 percent projected return. You figure that this is all you'll need to get everything you want from your wealth. But what if inflation, which was 3 percent when you put the plan together, jumps to 8 percent and stays near that level for years? Your "nominal" return of 8 percent will be just enough to break even net of inflation. What will happen then? Ask someone who retired in the 1970s. It ain't pretty.

If you believe as I do that inflation is a real threat to your long-term wealth growth plans, it follows that bond investing will be a whole new ball game. A very different outlook is needed for the investor and especially for the advisor. Why is this the case? A quick review of history and investment basics will explain.

For over a quarter century now, interest rates have been falling. As discussed earlier in this book, high-quality bond prices do not behave like stock prices. Stock prices are determined by everything from how profitable a company is, to what news events the company releases, to the desire of buyer and sellers (regardless of what the actual news is on the company). High-quality bonds are different. Their prices are determined largely by interest movements.

Now, interest rates can change due to a number of factors that are fundamentally based. But while a stock can go up or down regardless of the actual news (due to buying and selling forces of the market), bonds are more about mathematics. If interest rates go way down, bond prices are going to go up. Not maybe, not probably. They *will* go up.

This is what happened throughout most of the 1980s and 1990s with only temporary breaks such as in 1994 when the Fed raised interest rates seven times. If you were a bond manager in the past two decades, life was sweet. Your track record makes you look like a genius. In fact, it was actually the greatest bond bull market in modern history that made most bond managers appear heroic. If and when the party stops, it will hit many investors with a shock that will rival what we experienced when the tech stock bubble popped. I still think that the shock of seeing your high-quality bonds drop in value is a bigger emotional issue for most people than seeing stocks plunge.

High-quality bond funds are as bad an investment in a rising interest rate environment as they were a good investment in the falling rate period of the 1980s and 1990s. Based on the tremendous flows of cash into bond funds through most of 2009, I don't think the message is out there, at least not yet. And, like many bits of conventional wisdom, the message will spread very slowly.

The unfortunate fact is that if you look at how U.S. Treasury bonds of intermediate-term and long-term maturities (as defined in the very popular Ibbotson charts entitled "Stocks, Bonds, Bills and Inflation," which have been viewed by nearly every investment professional at some point in their career), you will find some five-year periods in the late 1970s and early 1980s in which long-term Treasuries lost over 40 percent, and intermediate-term Treasuries lost over 25 percent. Now, I am talking solely about the price component of the bonds, not the income. Back then, high interest rates served as a decent buffer to the falling bond prices. However, if bonds were to lose price value along the same lines today, the cushion from the low-interest-rate environment of the twenty-first century would be very narrow. The potential result is losses of great magnitude for a most unsuspecting group of investors—those who invest in U.S. Treasury securities!

Don't count on major Wall Street institutions to educate you on this. They are selling "the dream," and that includes making you believe that investments that performed well in the past will automatically perform well in the future. That is simply not always the case. In the case of high-quality bonds, the "new math" of this century could be very different from that of the late twentieth century. Don't get caught in the past if that happens. High-quality bond funds are a much riskier investment in a rising inflation environment than most investors realize.

- *U.S. deficits (government and consumer).* The hefty tab run up by the U.S. government over the years is a cause for some concern, and the media covers this regularly. The plight of the consumer is potentially much worse. Credit card debt became the currency of choice for many families. I marvel at how long people stretched the proverbial rubber band of borrowed money. When the band broke, this had a ripple effect on the financial system. It will continue to for a long time. This is not something to be in constant fear about; instead, it is something we know we have to consider when allocating assets in the twenty-first century.

  In particular, the U.S. dollar will be viewed with more skepticism for the next decade and probably beyond. The U.S. has created a long-term balance sheet nightmare for itself, and the rest of the world has been alerted to that fact. I feel confident that if I wrote another book in a few years, we would still be talking about how the U.S. dollar is not looked at as the untouchable premier currency around the globe. That creates some stomach upset for politicians and investors here, as well as companies that import goods. However, it provides substantial opportunities in the global stock, bond, and currency markets. The question is how to harness them. Regardless, this is another example of a change in the conventional wisdom allowing more adaptive investors to potentially flourish.

- *Global competitiveness.* Very simply, it's a global marketplace. Just look at communication systems, most prominently the Internet. What took days to become world news now takes seconds. That necessarily changes the way financial markets work. And it changes the way we must operate within them. This impacts not only stock markets, but bond markets as well. In particular, more lesser-developed countries are developing robust corporate bond markets to go with their existing stock markets. That provides more choice for investors, particular as those new markets get seasoned.

- *The retirement boom.* The Baby Boom generation has impacted our world at every phase of their lives. Now they are prepping for or entering the retirement phase. That has numerous implications for investing, but what they are is simply conjecture at this point.

- *More styles to choose from.* My friends who read this book will know immediately that I am *not* talking about clothes or cars. I'm referring to Wall Street's ingenuity. Here is where I truly applaud financial firms, especially the larger ones. As time has gone by, they have found ways for investors to take a stand in their portfolio on nearly any investment style, sector, or theme. Now, sometimes they charge an arm and a leg for it, and sometimes they sell it to clients as something beyond what it is. But for those of us that keep a close eye on the latest and greatest strategies and products, the freedom of choice that has developed is outstanding for investors—that is, as long as their advisors are looking out for the clients' best interests and not just their own.

- *Terrorism risk.* Without going into too much detail, one can no longer ignore this in today's environment. It is something that did not exist in a similar form in the glory days of the 1980s and 1990s. I worked in the World Trade Center on two different occasions in the 1980s and 1990s. I was trapped in one of the towers on the 97th floor in 1993 when terrorists attempted to blow up the building with a van filled with explosives in the basement. They missed that day, but then 9/11 occurred eight years later. We were all touched somehow when that fateful day came, and while the ongoing human impact in our daily lives is far more significant than how the terrorism issue impacts our wealth, the fact is that it is something that must be considered when allocating assets. That may be as simple as keeping a hedge in your portfolio at a slightly higher level than you might have 20 years ago. But it does have an impact,

even if years after that tragedy, the shock of that event has faded a bit.
- *Dealing with market volatility.* Simply put, volatility is the amount by which the price of an asset changes over some period of time. Everything in investing is cyclical, and the cycles can be days, weeks, months, years, or decades. Volatility is part of stock market investing and will always be.

From 1963 to 1998, the U.S. stock market's average daily price movement was six tenths of 1 percent. We studied the S&P 500's daily moves for the few years after 1998, and found that the average daily volatility was often more than double the historical average! Roughly speaking, that translates into a daily move of about 140 points on the Dow Jones Industrials. But if this is a fear generator, don't let the daily gyrations of the market disturb your dinner, sleep, or long-term investment goals.

Another important thing to remember about volatility is that it tends to be more consistent than performance for most asset classes. That is, while the investment return generated over a period of time by, say, large-cap growth stocks or international stocks will vary greatly, their level of volatility will stay more constant. Stocks as a group don't tend to stop moving around in price for periods of time. Over multiyear periods, stocks will nearly always be more volatile (variable) in their returns than bonds.

Volatility is something all successful long-term investors must endure to ultimately reach their goals. The key is to understand it, so you can deal with it rationally and keep your cool. In fact, you can turn the tables and use volatility to your advantage, if you know how. Later in the book, I describe in detail some ways to make volatility our friend instead of our enemy. It's not exactly playing on the fears of others, but there is a strong element of that. Simply put, having a strategy that is always prepared to exploit dramatic shifts in the market gives you a major advantage.

Where Does This Lead Us?

The conclusions from all of this are clear:

- Traditional asset allocation is not enough.
- Stocks alone are too volatile.

- Bond funds are no longer a reliable diversifier as the interest rate "tailwind" of more than 25 years ends.

Before you can even start to dissect specific markets and allocations of capital inside your portfolio, you have to recognize certain general tendencies of investors—tendencies that erode their hard-earned wealth. I have not conducted a formal study on this, but I have met with enough individual investors over the years that certain patterns become apparent. Those patterns persist from year to year, in good markets and bad, and among the super-wealthy, wealthy, and not-so-wealthy. It does not matter what your gender is. People are susceptible to certain greed versus fear reactions. We are all tempted to do things that, without our realizing it, will kill our portfolio if we don't arrest the behavior before it's too late. This chapter and this book are, at a minimum, designed to get your attention. At maximum, they are a pathway to getting what you want out of your money by avoiding the traps your friends and neighbors are likely to fall into. With that little "scared straight" speech out of the way, here we go. . . .

It's Time to Decide: Are You a Trader or an Investor?

The financial services industry has done much to empower individual investors in recent years. Many experienced investors now take advantage of the increased, timely information at their disposal. Many others have taught themselves how to create and execute an approach that makes sense for them. This is all great stuff.

However, this revolution now puts potentially dangerous tools in the hands of many inexperienced investors. Discount brokerage firm TD Ameritrade had a commercial encouraging investors to use the tools offered by the firm. At one point, the stoic actor Sam Waterston says to the camera, "You can do this!" I wish he'd say instead, "Some of you can do this."

It's not that people new to the markets can't profit from trading stocks. That would be foolish to say, since many have been successful. What is missing from many people's approach to the markets is their belief that they are *investors*. They are not investors; they are *traders*.

As Jerry Seinfeld would say, "not that there's anything wrong with that." However, it is critical to an investor's long-term financial health that he or she recognizes the difference. It's easy to be a trader when markets are continually moving up, or when volatile stocks make wild swings. However, even then, it's not easy to profit from it.

Trading can become much more difficult when the environment changes. That is when long-term, experienced, out-of-the-box-thinking investors will sleep peacefully, while traders try to figure out why the techniques that worked before are now blowing up. The key is to understand the difference between trading and investing (or a combination), choose the approach that you are most comfortable with, and go with it—without second-guessing yourself. It is said that one definition of an investor is "a disappointed speculator." Don't be one of those. As an investor, the more you live in the moment, the better the chances that your portfolio will suffer later (oh yeah, and when you least expect it).

Do You Think You Can Be Effective in Market Forecasting?

I wish I had a dollar for every market forecast I've ever seen. While predicting economic and market events has become something akin to a sporting event, sometimes a forecast can be useful. I advise you to consider the following anytime you read or hear a financial forecast, to avoid getting duped:

1. *What is the motivation of the forecaster?* If a small-cap stock fund manager tells you that small-cap stocks are a screaming buy, is that as reliable as someone whose livelihood isn't directly impacted by small-cap stock performance? To take this a giant step forward, did you ever notice how a decided majority of guests on financial TV shows are optimistic, all the time? Now you know why.
2. *Is that person speaking in absolutes, or leaving open the possibility that they are wrong?* Don't let someone's high level of conviction influence you too much. For more on this, see the first bullet point.
3. *What is the forecaster's experience?* In an era where any college kid, barber, or entertainer can get a web page and wax poetic about investing, you have to be careful.

Yes, making a lucky buy in a stock or a mutual fund that then experiences tremendous growth *does* occasionally happen. The key, however, is *luck.* To use a more modern example, someone who bought shares of Microsoft in the mid-1970s would probably be very pleased with their investment—however, there were many other computer software companies at the time—some of which seemed even more promising than Microsoft—whose investors ended up losing everything. Luck, more than wise selection, was the contributing factor to success.

Investment Football

Since the game of football is somewhat of a metaphor for much of the message of this book, let's start this chapter with an article I wrote in my *GreenThought$* newsletter at the height of the investor turmoil, in early 2009:

I have observed that investors and their financial advisors occasionally commit a variety of investment management "penalties."

While I certainly include myself among those who were imperfect in 2008, the fact remains that there is a certain perspective that all truly long-term investors must return to in times of financial distress. There is more to wealth management than guessing whether you should be "in the market" or "out of the market." And, simply saying "stay the course" when there may be serious issues in ones portfolio is a recipe for more of the same.

So, here is my list of official National Football League penalties—applied to investors. Don't get penalized; think your way through today's environment, or consult with those who can.

1. *False starts:* 5-yard penalty. It is human nature to be optimistic about the ability of the economy and the markets to eventually bounce back. I believe things will get better, and then much better in time. However, making an investment in something simply because it is way down in price is, like hope itself, not a strategy. Economies, markets, and human emotions recover in a "U-shaped" pattern, not a "V-shaped pattern." That is, they go through several little bipolar episodes before they return to sanity. Don't fight that, expecting to "get even" quickly. Focus on keeping losses short

term in nature and shallow in magnitude, and be opportunistic instead of aggressive. There are many investment approaches to accomplish this, and everyone needs to identify with one they are comfortable with. Still, those are words I live by.

2. *(Buy-and-) Holding:* 10-yard penalty. Just because your time horizon is long doesn't mean you can't sell something. As you can tell by the first penalty covered here, there is a balancing act to investing, especially today—practice diligent risk management, but don't just curl up in a shell and take no risk at all. If you do too much of the latter, you may get called for "intentional grounding" (5 yards plus loss of down) of what otherwise could be a productive portfolio.

3. *Delay of game:* 5-yard penalty. Going to cash or freezing up as an investor is fine if your current and forever goal is capital preservation to the exclusion of everything else, and inflation is not a concern to you. I congratulate those who timed their way into an all-cash portfolio last year. However, the risk of "sitting on the sidelines" for long periods of time is that you will forever be trying to pick your spots to "get back into the market." That is a skill that is tough to master over and over, and for those with long-term investment objectives, it can be as much of a detriment as being too aggressive. I raise my cash position as a "weapon" and portfolio hedge quite often; it's the all-or-nothing scenarios I am warning against here.

4. *Pass interference:* 15-yard penalty. I am calling this one on the mainstream media and the big, impersonal investment firms. In their supposed efforts to "help" investors, they continue to present a message that has become a cliché, but to the detriment of many, oversimplifies some general investment concepts. Examples of this oversimplified advice include the following. I have summarized the other side of this conventional wisdom here as well:

   a. Buy low-cost mutual funds—in tough markets, net return, not cost is what matters.

   b. Diversify your portfolio—yet many seemingly diversified portfolios are really not.

   c. Style purity—restricting a portfolio manager to specific market segments (small cap, international, etc.) can lead to the investment equivalent of a hamstring injury in football. That is, the manager's abilities are restricted due to lack of mobility.

5. *Clipping . . . bond coupons:* 15-yard penalty. The credit crisis has changed the bond game, maybe for a long time. Gone are the days where one confidently built a "carefree" laddered maturity portfolio of high-quality corporate or municipal bonds. The bond market will likely return to its "old reliable" status again at some point. For now, however, low CD yields, suspect rating agencies, and the general fear of risk in the bond market is akin to relying on a slumping place-kicker to win a game with a long field goal into the wind. It may work out but you are not as comfortable about it as you used to be. That should cause the resourceful investor and advisor to look for different ways to manage the conservative part of an overall portfolio.

6. *Illegal formation:* 5-yard penalty. Thousands of people hold themselves out as "asset allocators." I am one of them. However, asset allocation is an art as well as a science. It is not simply a neat computer program in the hands of an MBA, or a "target-date" mutual fund that purports to tell you today how you should allocate your assets for the next 30 years. Those all sound good and look pretty, but may not get the job done.

7. *Too many men on the field:* 5-yard penalty. I have read recently that the lack of trust in Wall Street will lead some investors to split their pot among several financial advisors. In my opinion this works only if you can truly identify the unique role played by each advisor in the total portfolio. Otherwise, you are just collecting advisors like coins or stamps (or stocks, as some overdiversified investors do).

Getting advice from too many sources often leads to uncoordinated advice, unless the client is willing to be their own investment "quarterback." As with football, in the financial game, quarterback is the toughest position to play.

8. *Offsides:* 5-yard penalty. Investors probably feel that they have been on the "wrong side of the market" lately. The conclusion they reach is to either hope the stock market goes up or sit it out until it does. Both approaches should send yellow penalty flags flying! A solution I have found that may cut investment losses and emotions, thereby keeping more players

in the game, is to incorporate the use of securities that simulate short positions (which benefit from prices of a group of stocks or bonds going down) alongside their traditional "long" positions (i.e., buying something and profiting if it goes up). This is a portfolio feature that matters less when we are "on offense"—such as a long bull market. However, simply adding the potential to use the short side of the market when conditions demand it can insulate your portfolio like those portable heaters the players use on the sidelines during December games in Green Bay.

9. *Roughing the passer:* 15-yard penalty. Taking it all out on your advisor (i.e., your "investment quarterback") when they are trying to manage to your ultimate objectives. Time horizons and risk tolerance are serious stuff. Yet sometimes the investor profiling process is done formally, but neither the investor nor the advisor gets the most realistic picture of what the client's specific need for risk management is. In times like this, an investor may be tempted to convince themselves to look for advice from new sources. Sometimes that makes sense, but often it's one of those "grass is always greener" scenarios. In other words, it may appear that whoever the incumbent advisor is, they are automatically considered expendable. That's when the client has to remember what drew them to their advisor in the first place, and whether those reasons are still valid. Often, they are. I could have called this one a penalty for "unnecessary roughness" instead.

10. *Unsportsmanlike conduct:* 15-yard penalty. Anyone in the investment business that provides advice not in the best interest of the client gets flagged on this one.

So, that's "Investment Football." While these "penalties" exist, as with football itself they are setbacks, not game-breakers. If you accumulate a lot of penalties, it will make it tougher to win the game. However, if investors and their advisors work together to cut down on these progress inhibitors, they stand a much better chance of the scoreboard's turning in their favor. To do so, you must, as the pros say, "play 60 minutes"—no big letdowns, stay focused, be innovative, and give your all on every play. For investors and advisors alike, that is the path to victory.

More Bad Habits to Kick

Now, not every warning to investors can be related to football. What follows is my list of some behaviors I believe can also result in self-inflicted wounds to the investor and his or her advisor (if the advisor recommended the action). That does not mean that these approaches never work—in fact, several people I have talked to brag about how they did not lose money in 2008, since they were in cash the whole year. That's assuming they are all telling the truth.

One thing I enjoy about managing money in today's techno-savvy world is that the investor can see my performance every business day. In other words, I can't fake my performance. So, for those reasons, and because "Investing for Idiots" is already taken by someone else, here is a list of investor habits I'd suggest you avoid.

An Obsession with Risk Avoidance

Risk avoidance is a natural part of any investor's approach, but taken to any extreme, it is not often very helpful to your overall goals. In addition to indexing, many investors believe that staying clear of high-risk investments will protect them indefinitely. This is simply not true. "Conservative" investments such as utility stocks and low-volatility hedge funds are also fallible. For example, utility stocks, once thought of as the "safe" money, have experienced some wild price swings in recent years. The lesson here: nearly every investment carries risk and will experience some volatility. The challenge is to offset the negative characteristics of certain parts of your portfolio with other styles that allow the entire portfolio to succeed most of the time, and to keep the losing periods to a minimum. I have shown investors over and over that you do not have to invest aggressively to earn solid, productive, long-term returns. However, you have to remove the money from under your mattress to have a chance. Later in the book, I will provide what I think is a meaningful guide to "risk management," which will allow you to feel empowered against market risk and volatility, instead of being fearful of it.

"I Could Have Done Better Having My Money in the Bank"

Investing is making an educated guess about what will perform most in line with your objectives over your time horizon. Either you make those educated guesses and follow them along, or you have an advisor do it for you. Do you want to do the educated guessing and the research that goes with it, or do you want to pay someone to do it for/with you?

I think that the reason many clients come to an independent firm like ours is that they feel that their broker did not take this "educated guess" role seriously. Instead, the client had a salesperson whose interests were more aligned with the firm than the client.

I have also seen many people come to our firm and to other independents from trust companies. In this case, it seems that the advisor there was unwilling to deviate from what the firm was doing for thousands of other clients—there was little regard for the particular issues in the investor's financial life.

To me, investing in the twenty-first century will be about grinding out return where and when it is available; opportunities may not be plentiful like in the 1990s. The key to achieving goals will be a *flexible* game plan using a wide variety of resources (i.e., several different investment strategies). Want to simply put all of your money in an S&P index fund and endure the ebbs and flows of the market, or sock it away in whatever asset class had the best year last year (a.k.a. the "hot dot")? That's an educated guess I don't agree with, yet many individual investors have done that. More power to them, but I think it will be much tougher than that to accomplish what you want.

The "Seen One, Seen 'Em All" Rule

"I'm not investing in mutual funds anymore. Did you hear what those bums did at ABC and XYZ mutual fund company?" If you are in the health care field and you are reading this, let's hope the same logic doesn't apply to your industries. Is every doctor guilty of malpractice, or is every dentist a clone of that dentist whose office was also his car? Or are those people who diluted the pills taken by cancer patients a symbol for all of you? I doubt it. Don't generalize when it comes to investing. That is the easy path, but often the most disappointing one.

De-Worse-ification

To start with, there is the issue of what I call "de-worse-ification." I believe that the traditional idea of diversification is overdone. I see so many portfolios that started with the idea of not having all the eggs in one basket, and apparently decided that starting a basket factory was a better idea. In other words, they took it too far, and now have what is no longer a portfolio but a "collection of securities." They and their advisors think they are doing what is necessary, but they take it too far. Maybe it's the unending supply of investment strategies, but here's the rub—diversification is about reducing volatility and risk through the addition of investment styles whose characteristics are different from the rest of the portfolio. Diversification is *not* simply adding more and more assets and styles with no strategy or direction. Adding more apples to your apples doesn't make fruit salad; it makes a bigger pile of apples! And at some point the apples go rotten, and there's nothing to save you. Similarly, there will be periods where the commonly used approach to diversification and asset allocation set families back for years.

Performance Contests

I have been asked a few times in my career to participate in a "performance contest" in order to gain more of a client's wealth. That is, the client said they would divide their money between two firms and whoever did the best over the following year would get the other half of the money.

When a client invites their advisor to compete in a performance contest, no one wins. This is a lot like going to a top-quality restaurant, having a meal you don't like, and deciding never to go again.

By the way, if the "winning" firm in that performance contest gets the other half of your money, what assurance do you have that they will be the superior firm next year? Answer: none. So next time you feel the urge to make your portfolio's return the subject of a contest or race, turn on the television and watch a ballgame or a cooking show, or read a book. And when it's time to analyze your portfolio, spend your energy on understanding more about what's in it, how it addresses your specific goals, and how prepared it is for a variety of market conditions.

Shooting the Weak Performer

Different investment styles perform differently in different market environments. That's why I have advocated a total portfolio approach using what I call a twenty-first-century asset allocation approach. Think back no further than 2007. What worked for investors that year slaughtered them in 2008. If you had been in a performance contest, the contest "winner" in 2007 likely would have ruined many years of the client's hard work just one year later. Put another way, performance of an investment over any period of time is *not* a verdict on that investment's effectiveness. More likely, it is a reflection of that investment style's behavior in the type of market environment that existed during the measurement period.

I can cite many examples of this over my career, but I'll choose one. In early 2007, a few investors were concerned that one of the positions in their portfolio was losing money when everything else was going up. This pattern continued for months. One investor even went so far as to say they had looked up the fund's rating on Morningstar, and it had received that estimable fund analysis firm's lowest rating. Why, they asked, would we ever want to own such a fund?

Of course, it is also possible that an investment manager is in a slump. It happens to every athlete (okay, Tiger Woods didn't ever have a slump, but as we now know, he had some extra help in avoiding them). In addition, the reasons that an investment may deliver mediocre performance over a short stretch of time (yes, a year is short) are not all bad ones.

More likely, the explanation for a "weak performer" within a portfolio has to do with the role that the particular fund played in the overall portfolio. The fund's goal was to short stocks of companies that its managers believed were fundamentally flawed, making their current price level unsustainable. They were trying to find ways to make money when the value of these companies was discovered by the broad market, thus profiting from their downfall. Through much of 2007, it didn't matter what stocks you shorted; they probably did not go down. It was only once the market recognized major changes in the global financial system that those stocks started to decline in price, raising the price of that fund.

The fund was a part of one of our strategies because it represented a way to offset the risk inherent in a portfolio that, at the time, was generally positioned for a rising stock market. It was a "hedge" on the rest of the portfolio. When the market turned down in late 2007, and continued to drop through 2008 and into early 2009, guess which fund was the star of that portfolio? You guessed it—the much-maligned fund that just a year earlier had been denigrated by some of its investors.

The lesson here: if you know why you own every mutual fund in your portfolio and what you expect from it, you can focus on whether the performance of that fund is in line with what you would expect in a particular marking period you evaluate. Evaluating based on what you expect from a fund within your overall portfolio, instead of drawing broad conclusions from results in a particular small time frame, will help you avoid "shooting the weak performer." Sometimes they are weak for a reason, and that reason is exactly why you, the long-term investor, own it in the first place!

The bottom line is this: portfolio management is not a game, but it *is* a team. Constructing a portfolio involves identifying investments that each play a role in your ultimate success. In some years, any one of those investments will be the hero; the next year, it could be your only negative return in the bunch. If your goal, like many of our clients, is to earn more consistent, lower-volatility returns instead of simply tracking the ups and downs of the markets, your portfolio should have a mix of investments that in some ways offset or complement each other.

Don't get me wrong—there is a time and a reason to pull the trigger on an investment, but it is *not* because of short-term underperformance.

"Rearview Mirror Investing"

This is one of the most blatant violations of the rules investors should beware of. Maybe there should be a sticker on lists of recent top-performing mutual funds: "Warning: you may be too late to enjoy any of this!" While recent performance may be attractive, the numbers alone do not tell the whole story. What drove the performance? Was it an overall tendency in the market, an indication of the success of the investing methodology of the fund, or the result of random events and blind luck? The most important question regarding performance is whether the conditions that led to such performance are likely to continue. Is performance sustainable? This is where detailed and professional analysis comes into play.

This century began with two markets: a tech boom and a non-tech bear market. The impact this had on investors' approach to the stock market is striking, yet worrisome. Those who rode the

Internet bandwagon from the beginning profited handsomely. Others joined in later because they felt they had missed out. This is what we call "Rearview Mirror Investing." A driver who looks only at what's behind is unprepared for what's on the road ahead.

This can be a dangerous game. The media, by focusing tremendous attention on what is popular, helps to create these emotions in us. To me, it is another one of the hard-coded investor behaviors from the learning period of the 1980s and 1990s that must be unlearned for you to be successful. As a friend once told me: if CNBC came on the air and said "buy quality stocks, hold them for the long term, and have a nice day," they'd be off the air in a week!

The point is that diversification still has a place in everyone's portfolio. You may want to bet on yesterday's winner, but the stock market has shown time and again that things have a way of frustrating the most people they possibly can. If and when that happens again, you'll want your portfolio to be ready for it.

The Other Enemy

This chapter covered what I call "The Issues and the Enemy"—that is, the issues you need to grapple with as a twenty-first-century investor, and the patterns of behavior that I believe get investors in trouble. So, sometimes the enemy is the market or some other type of inanimate object that you can't really control anyway. However, sometimes the enemy is you. I hope that by taking in all of what you read in this chapter, I can help you prevent yourself from being another of the investment world's long list of victims.

In my career, I have seen that very often, the "enemy" of the investor and the independent financial advisor is the behemoths of Wall Street. The next chapter will round out our discussion of what you need to know before we plunge into the approach I suggest using in the twenty-first century.

5

Wall Street's Bull

Here is what I feel is the standard chronology for a Wall Street disaster:

- A good product idea is developed.
- That product idea starts to get popular with financial advisors.
- Product companies begin mass-producing the product, each trying to "one-up" the others.
- Increasingly innovative but more complex varieties of the product become available.
- The media starts to poke holes in the now-ubiquitous product.
- Product producers and users insist the media and other detractors are wrong (and this gets less press coverage than the stories that show the product in a positive light—that is, a star is born, but the star's flaws are downplayed).
- Most of the investing public (including advisors) either don't know about the potential pitfalls of the product or ignore those risks.
- The risks are eventually realized, and massive losses of money and "face" occur.
- Investors and their advisors vow never to be fooled like this again.

Past examples include 1970's oil and gas partnerships, junk bonds in the 1980s, and, more recently, collateralized debt obligations (CDOs), mortgage-backed securities (MBSs), and other leveraged investments. Despite the long history of investor disappointment, the Wall Street firms keep cranking out products and ideas that investors fall for, just like Charlie Brown trying to kick that football while Lucy holds it—until she pulls it away at the last minute. Rather than simply walking around feeling that Wall Street is a casino run by a bunch of greedy pit bosses, it's okay to look in the mirror, realize that you do not have to be as gullible as the next dude, and educate yourself about what I affectionately call "Wall Street's Bull."

Shortcuts and Overkill

Much of my first book was devoted to identifying potentially damaging conflicts of interest at brokerage firms, investment product manufacturers, and certain types of financial advisory outlets. A lot of what I warned about actually did come to pass in 2008, and some of the earlier chapters of this book focused you on the causes, results, and lessons of that year for investors. In this chapter, I will complete my updated identification and purging of past sins of investors, their advisors, and the Wall Street firms that often influence both of them. Then, we'll introduce you to your new investment "playbook" so we can look forward and get you on track for the rest of your investment life.

There is no doubt that an explosion of new financial products has taken place. And, yes, some of the products themselves have exploded, too. Take the so-called "alternative investments," which I will discuss again later in this book. They come in many varieties, and they have gotten so "hot" in the financial advisor marketplace, they are starting to take on characteristics of investment product "bubbles" of the past. For instance, hedge funds-of-funds seem to be losing their popularity. In the meantime, product creators are one-upping each other, creating leveraged exchange-traded funds (ETFs) that to some of us simply look like gambling tools designed to avoid taking out a margin loan. Commodity funds and ETFs are everywhere, and, as of late 2009, new ones were born every month.

You have to ask yourself: why the frenzy to pursue alternative investments? As I often say to advisors who invest with us on behalf of their clients: we all know that our job is to do what is prudent. However, it is also important to do what is *necessary*. I see signs that, as in the past, financial advisors are being given temptation to go beyond what is necessary to pursue the objective of adding low-correlation alternative investments to their client portfolios.

Examples of both "shortcuts" and "overkill" by Wall Street and its participants are numerous. Let's now focus on a few that are increasingly troublesome to you, in the opinion of my investment team and me.

Taking the Shortcut

When my kids were younger, there was nothing they enjoyed more than hearing that we are "taking the shortcut" to reach our destination. Even if it were a five-minute trip, they loved it. In fact, if my wife and I simply told them we were taking the shortcut to get somewhere, Jordann, Tyler, and Morgan would get a great sense of satisfaction. While shortcuts are great when you're taking your kids someplace, they can be disastrous in the investing world.

Wall Street has notoriously developed shortcuts in creating and managing portfolios. Products have been created for the sole purpose of being easy to sell. While an argument can be made that the investor has been benefited because there are more investment opportunities than ever before, the financial advisor community has been given tools to make them lazy. The problem is: how do you sort the good from the bad? Some clients fall for a good presentation; the more educated ones will realize there is no substance.

Brokerage firms, trust companies, and bank investment advisory firms also take shortcuts. But they are often not enjoyable for you, the client. Why are they taking shortcuts? Very simply, they do so to increase their profit margin at your expense.

They are not doing it with malicious intentions. On the contrary, they do it to make their businesses as efficient as possible. It is tough to keep thousands of brokers in hundreds of offices around the country in sync. And many brokerage firms, trust companies, and bank advisors are part of publicly traded companies. If you are running one of those companies, you are there to do what is in the best interests of the shareholders—this is exactly what most Wall Street CEOs say when they are interviewed about their businesses.

If the business increases profits substantially quarter after quarter, year after year, the stock price of that company you run will likely go up. This brings all kinds of good news for the CEO, their board of directors, and their shareholders. The stock price rises, shareholders make money, the CEO earns a ton as your company stock options become more valuable, and the company gets more popular with investors. This is all fantastic news—**for the CEO and the shareholders, but not necessarily for the clients of that firm!**

Are You Being Advised or Sold To?

In the October 2004 issue of *Investment Advisor* magazine, Dan Wheeler, the director of global financial services for Dimensional Fund Advisors, wrote an article, "House of Games," which sums up this dilemma. He wrote that

> . . . the problem with seeking professional investment help is that all too often the person sitting across from the investor as an "advisor" is there to make a sale . . . unfortunately too many people think that Wall Street brokerage firms are there to provide investors with good advice designed to help them reach their financial goals.

That's powerful stuff. Yet in my experience, having worked at brokerage firms, trust companies, and banks, and despite my generally positive disposition, I'm inclined to agree with him. I have just seen, over and over again, how investors do not get what they really want from their advisors—straightforward providers of advice and direction, who customize their thinking to that of each individual client. As time goes on, I see more and more of the industry truly acting as "fiduciaries" to their clients, and that is great to see. But there is a long way to go until investors' objectives and those of their advisors totally match up. That is why surveys of investors in 2009 suggested that most investors were not satisfied with their advisors.

You must ask yourself: in an industry where many are rated by their employers based primarily on the revenue they bring to the firm as "producers," and not how much better off their clients are for being with them, is there not an obvious disconnect between the needs of the clients and the way those needs are being addressed? I think there is, and I also think that many financial advisors have figured this out over the years, and rightly decided to start independent firms. What was once a small minority of the professional financial advisor population has grown into a giant that now rivals the size of the traditional brokerage industry.

Independent advisors come in all shapes and sizes, but in my opinion, they are the ones who "get it"—they treat the client as a teammate, not an opponent, and see their role as being the client's advocate, representative, and interpreter within an increasingly complex investment world. That also makes them much more likely to adopt the type of twenty-first-century asset allocation thinking that this book espouses. Furthermore, they do so without making it appear that the client is getting something they are not. Shortcuts and overkill by Wall Street firms increase the chance of the client's later feeling fooled, and feeling like a fool. Independent firms will, in my opinion, continue to be the winners in that battle for the client's affections because they are far less likely to allow that to happen.

Conventional Wisdom: Not So Smart

The other issue in the financial services area that causes confusion for today's investor is the way the industry clings to the common wisdom of past eras, even when conditions have changed dramatically. Without getting into too much detail here, there was a study done about 30 years ago that determined that asset allocation was by far the most significant determinant of investment success. That is, if you have the right balance of stocks, bonds, and cash in your portfolio, your probability of success is much greater. Many a financial product advertisement references this study in one form or another. This is, however, somewhat deceptive.

Simply put, that study does *not* apply to many of today's investors. To me, while asset allocation is important, it is not as important as having someone in your corner to whom you can talk about what you want out of life, and who has the experience and skills to craft for you a strategy that maximizes the probability that your money will get you there. Investors don't come to advisors because they want a stock or bond portfolio. They do so because they have accumulated money; life costs money and they want to make the most effective use of their money. The investments chosen are simply a means to an end, not the end itself. I read an article by an advisor who described this quite well. He said that his company exists "because the world is more complex—and we're all just one minute away from chaos. What we do is a risk management strategy for our lives." Investing is not really about what hot stock you just bought or the sleek hedge fund you snuck into while others missed out.

But too many advisors miss this as they mature in the business. Instead, they become part of the industry machine that says things like "here's a diversification plan for everyone" and other solutions we refer to as "mass-customized advice." Be wary of firms and advisors who take shortcuts with your money.

Fear of the unknown is why some clients stay with a broker or bank instead of going with an independent firm. But this is an irrational fear. If renaissance mariners had been unable to overcome their fear of the unknown, we would still believe the world is flat; and if clients cannot overcome their fear of stepping outside the traditional investment box, their returns may be just as flat.

As someone who is by nature a strategic thinker, a detail-seeker (you know, the kind of person who wants to know how the watch is made, not just what time it is), this concept was something I had to learn myself as I grew up in the business. This was the most important thing I learned in the industry during my twenties. No matter how much your firm says "do this for your clients," advisors must resist the temptation to put anyone else's agenda ahead of their clients'.

A Shocking Fact

When you first learn about the stock market, you are liable to be taught that the long-term average annual return of stocks is about 10 percent. That figure is based on a widely followed, documented history of the U.S. stock market (as measured by the S&P 500 stock index) by Ibbotson Associates, an esteemed research firm. Their data starts in 1926 and is updated each year. Ibbotson does terrific work, but recently I stumbled upon a stray fact that really challenges this conventional wisdom.

The stock market at that stage of the "Roaring Twenties" was not unlike that of the late 1990s. In fact, it took nearly two decades for the market to recover from the damage that occurred during the crash of that period. This is just one of many historical facts that has been brushed aside by the investment industry because it does not sell well to the public.

I'm here to tell you that the 10 percent stock market average is a myth. More importantly, the fact that it is a myth does not have to impact one's ability to reach his or her individual wealth goals. Why not? Because if you focus on making money and not being tied to the allure of the market averages, you can escape the fate of those who started investing at a point in history that just happened to be untimely for a "buy-and-hold" type of investor (such as the end of 2007). Look no further than the series of price charts on the Dow Jones Industrial Average presented earlier.

Overlap

Many investment firms have built their success by essentially spinning off similar versions of one of their products. For instance, if their original growth stock fund becomes popular, they come out with another growth fund. Oh, they find some way to make it appear quite different from the original, but it usually isn't. Over time, the trained eye will find that a mutual fund family offers many funds that look, act, and perform very similarly.

Why would a company do this? In my opinion, it's to create the impression that you can buy several of their funds in the name of diversification. After all, if you have all of your money in one of their funds, even though that fund may own 150 stocks, Wall Street may try to tell you that you are not diversified. After all, you own only one fund. So, to help you diversify and capitalize on your positive opinion of them (you must have a positive opinion since you have your money there), they offer you a different fund.

This sounds reasonable except for one thing: there are only so many ways to invest in growth stocks or value stocks, or stocks at all, using traditional approaches. What this points out is that there is much homework to be done. In the money management business, we call that homework on securities, funds, and managers "due diligence." We in the industry pay professional analysts good money to slice and dissect performance results and qualitative as well as quantitative factors about investment vehicles. A "do-it-yourself" investor would find it extremely difficult to replicate the depth of intelligence we gather.

Now, I'm not saying that all funds that target investment in traditional asset classes are lousy investments. I'm simply pointing out what I've gravitated to over the years when it comes to selecting investments for the equity portion of my clients' portfolios:

- There are managers that have consistently provided "alpha," or returns above the market return.

- Those managers are typically not found at the largest, best-known firms.

The conclusion: diversification means owning different assets that have very different characteristics. Investing in several funds that are essentially clones of each other does not satisfy that definition.

10 Investment Ideas that Still Don't Work

In the last two chapters, I described a wide range of investor tendencies and habits, in hopes of steering you clear of what I believe are common mistakes that inhibit the growth and preservation of wealth. Many of these focused more on misperception of facts as opposed to misdirection due to Wall Street firms' tactics. You have probably figured out by now that I am not the type to keep quiet when I think that Wall Street is taking the "bull" too far, so to speak.

It is extremely troubling to me that some of the same patterns we have seen lead to destruction of capital hit the radar screen again and again. They come in some new disguises, but I recognize them, and thus feel compelled to point them out.

I'd be happy to be wrong on all of these concerns, and settle for having simply made you more informed and a bit more wary of Wall Street's "bull." Right or wrong, I hope you recognize that by pointing out these potentially poisonous apples in your own Garden of Eden, I "have your back" when it comes to interpreting Wall Street's increasingly confusing and complex signals and temptations. To that end, here is a brief explanation of my top 10 investment ideas and approaches that have not worked much in the past and *still* don't work today:

1. *"130/30" investment strategies.* These mutual funds and ETFs fake you into thinking you are getting something you are not. In theory, they attempt to buy stocks that the manager expects to go up in price. Then, they borrow against 30 percent of their asset pool to short stocks they don't like. Frankly, if they stopped right there, I think it would be a credible product. But they don't. They then take the 30 percent worth of proceeds from the short sales (when you short

stock, you borrow stock from a brokerage firm, your account is credited with cash until you decide to close your short position, at which point you pay back whatever that short position is worth at that point). The result of all of this is that 130 percent of your investment is in what the manager feels are the "good stocks" and 30 percent worth of your investment is "sold short" in "bad stocks." In theory, this means your manager's stock-picking skills on both the long and short sides of the market are put into play for your benefit. There's one problem, though: their skills are not that great. The results of these funds have been anywhere from mediocre to atrocious. To make matters worse, they are often sold to investors as some sort of hedge fund strategy for the little guy. That does not hold water. Why not? Because your net exposure to the stock market is about zero (130 percent long – 30 percent short). That means that the manager has to survive based solely on their stock-picking skills on both sides of the market. As we learned from the rise and fall of the hedge fund industry, the key to success was often more about leveraging up one's portfolio than about great stock picking. Thus, the investor is left with a portfolio they have been led to believe is a hedge fund–like vehicle. Then, when they see the results, they realize that at best, they are overpaying for an index fund.

2. *Leveraged ETFs.* At the height of their popularity in mid-2009, I warned my audience through the *GreenThought$* newsletter that leveraged ("juiced") ETFs might be the next Wall Street catastrophe. My timing was pretty good, as a few weeks later, regulators started to question these products when used for anything beyond day-trading. These so-called "juiced" ETFs (a reference to the boost athletes get from steroid use) appeared to be the next "gotta have it" product. That is always a warning sign, and I am very glad that increased regulatory scrutiny is now applied.

When I first heard about leveraged ETFs, I thought I was standing in a Starbucks store. "I'd like a double-short S&P mid-cap exchange-traded fund, please." While we used them a bit in our early days of ETF work, we stopped using them so as to avoid what we feel may be a "Grande" mishap for our clients.

My colleague and expert market technical analyst Michael Kahn follows ETFs closely, and he researched the leveraged variety for his *Quick Takes Pro* daily newsletter. He believes the bottom line is this:

> These things decay over time whether you are right or wrong. I feel the answer lies in the same simple mathematical rule that concerns how to recover from losses in the stock market. In other words, if you have experienced big losses in the market, even if you correctly predict the S&P 500 will crash, buy an ETF that rises twice as fast as the S&P falls, you can still come out a loser.

How can this be? As a quick example, if you lost 40 percent in 2008 but gained 20 percent so far in 2009, you would only be back to $72 for every $100 you started with (not $80 as some might expect).

It's the same thing with leveraged ETFs, whether or not they are the type that allow for hyperparticipation in up or down markets. A fellow named Matt Hougan, in an article for a publication called *IndexUniverse*, found that twice-leveraged investments will deliver no more than 130 to 150 percent of an index return over the long run. That still may sound great, but when you consider that you were probably expecting much more, and that in many cases people use these ETFs as hedging devices, you can see where you might likely fall short (so to speak).

Still, for very short-term traders, I believe leveraged ETFs can play a useful role, assuming the investor knows how to use them. In our opinion, this is not like putting a kid behind the wheel of a Honda Civic; it's more like strapping them into a Ferrari—it's not for beginners. Investopedia.com, a very helpful website for investment basics, explains leveraged ETFs very simply: *A leveraged ETF does not amplify the annual returns of an index; instead it follows the daily changes.* Where some people get fooled is by expecting that the 2:1 or 3:1 ratio that the ETF delivers on a single day will also be realized over their personal holding period (weeks, months, years). This will be an ongoing industry debate as the proliferation of these leveraged ETFs continues. My advice: stay tuned, stay educated, and stay off the juice.

3. *Hypothetical track records as a primary means of promoting one's future performance potential.* I have seen rampant use of performance records that may seem very legitimate to the casual viewer who takes a quick read, and evaluates manager performance statistics at face value. However, historically there has been a great deal of rule bending in this area. You should always read the disclaimers in any performance report from a money manager, though I will note that the mutual fund industry is tightly regulated in this area, so that is not where the problem lies. The separate-account industry does include firms that have achieved their "results" through computer simulation, back-testing, what-if scenarios, and other means that lack one critical element: they are not actual accounts where actual money was invested. Or they include actual accounts, but in way that allows the manager leeway to "cherry-pick" one or more accounts as being "representative" of their investment method. You can believe whatever you want, but I will tell you that the number one reason my firm went through the arduous task of getting our separate account track record audited according to Global Investment Performance Standards (GIPS) is that, in our mind, it eliminates all questions of whether the data and conclusions we present to investors are somehow compromised. If it is GIPS compliant, it isn't compromised. Or, as one famous episode of the hit show *Seinfeld* ended, if the numbers are GIPS, "they're real." I'll leave it to you to judge whether they are also "spectacular."

4. *"Hot tips" on investments.* Need I say more? Sure, some of these work out, but from many anecdotal situations I have been told about, most of them don't. They don't work out because the investor focuses on the opportunity for instant wealth instead of if and where it fits into their overall portfolio. I am a big fan of "taking big shots with small amounts of money," but I leave it to you to figure out whether that proverbial fish farm in South Dakota is something you should be tooling around with. If so, don't sink 50 percent of your capital into it.

5. *Tactical portfolio management, when used in isolation (i.e., as a strategy in itself).* Remember when you were a kid and you told your parents you did something because your friends were

doing it? At least once in your life, your parents probably responded with "just because everyone is doing it, that doesn't make it right." Then they muttered something about "if your friends jumped off the Brooklyn Bridge. . . . "

Wall Street is often a copycat business. Someone comes up with a decent strategic idea for investment portfolios, and it works for a while. Then, all of a sudden, many other firms start doing something similar, or something that seems similar. Two results typically occur: First, it turns out that the original idea was helpful during certain market conditions, which helps the "early adopters." Meanwhile, the "Johnny-come-lately" types enjoy only the tail end of the success. Market conditions eventually change, and the idea, while still useful, is not practical as a core strategy. Then, clients get discouraged because their advisors always seem to be one step behind, and they get caught up with the "herd." And the herd never wins for long. Some of the most well-known investor sentiment indicators have shown over time that buying high and selling low, instead of the reverse, is way too fashionable.

In 2009, largely in reaction (or overreaction) to the events of 2008, I saw signs that this was happening again. This time the hot topic was "tactical asset allocation" (TAA).

The website businessdictionary.com defines the word *tactical* as "involving or pertaining to actions, ends, or means that are immediate or short-term in duration, and/or lesser in importance or magnitude, than those of a strategy or a larger purpose." So, it follows that TAA is a way to invest for short-term gains in market areas that you don't plan to invest in for the long-term—it's not trading, but it's not your main focus, either. Despite this, many have tried and failed to achieve good long-term results relying solely on tactical strategies (read: hedge fund business—implosion).

The preceding definition notes that tactical business strategies are short term but also that they are less important than the overall strategy. They are more of a "role player" in your portfolio. Their role may be more important during some periods (read: treacherous markets).

Tactical strategies have been around for a long time, and we have used them in moderation across our portfolio work. They were particularly helpful in 2008, when the stock market's plunge rewarded those who refrained from "buy-and-hold" strategies. With investors still stinging from the events of last year, it's not surprising that financial advisors and product producers are filling the air with talk of "you have to do this tactical asset allocation thing" or something of that sort. It's typical human nature that capital preservation is sexy on the heels of a huge bear market. Also, the idea of jumping around the markets to profit here, then there, then somewhere else is always sexy to investors. There is only one problem—in the vast majority of cases, the success is not sustainable on a wide scale.

So the message to you is simply this: tactical asset allocation is best used as a tool within a larger portfolio, not as a long-term strategic commitment. That is how I view the use of TAA in my portfolio management and asset allocation work. It can help reduce the volatility of returns, but if you rely too heavily on it, you may just miss the bull market that forms while you are still responding to the last bear market. Fighting the last war is not a strategy for success. It's also highly tax inefficient.

As an industry peer has said, people always want to own what they wish they had owned last year. Need a reminder? Did you own a tech-heavy portfolio in 1999? Did you own commodity-related investments last spring? Many investors ran to these then-popular spots, realizing later that they arrived just before the party ended. This is investor emotion at its finest.

This begs the question: is TAA about to revert to its true role as a tool and not a total portfolio strategy, or is the rash of new tactical investment products (including the dreaded aforementioned leveraged ETFs) a sign that TAA is a useful tool but nothing more? Sure looks like it to me. Or, to put it another way, "bull markets smell like this." When risk avoidance is the hot idea, it is time to start thinking about how to position for the next bull cycle. I prefer to focus more of my energies on an investment process I believe can be applied continuously and sustainably through all parts of the market cycle. Tactical work is a part of that, but it is more of a side dish than the main course.

6. *All-or-nothing investment approaches,* such as "I am in the market" or "I got out of the market." Time after time we see this

backfire on investors and their advisors. I think of investing as shades of gray, not black-or-white decisions. More on this later in the book.

7. *Hanging on every economic release as if it is make-or-break information for your retirement goals.* I refer to this as "hanging by a Fed" and I caution against it. Same for the majority of "insights" that come from financial television. Those insights have an agenda, so be careful.

8. *A glut of "me-too" investment products.* Recent examples include the explosion of absolute return funds, managed futures vehicles, and ETFs based on contrived indexes. As with hedge funds a few years ago, people want to buy what they wish they had bought last year. Product producers know that and they feed off of it—and off of you if you are not careful.

9. *Assuming that bigger is better when it comes to mutual fund product providers.* The biggest fund companies have several drawbacks that often make them less appealing than investing with established, more entrepreneurial fund managers and fund companies.

10. *Thinking your portfolio is doing great because you are way up this year after being way down last year.* The problem is that when trying to bounce back from a large hit to your portfolio, the math works against you. For instance, if you lost about what the S&P 500 Index lost in 2008 (37 percent), you started 2009 with your portfolio worth 63 cents on the dollar versus the start of 2008. If you again matched the market's performance in 2009 (about 26 percent), you grew that 63 cents to about 79 cents. That's a nice improvement, but you are still nowhere near where you started at the end of 2007. This is why we try to be so diligent on risk—the big drop in value is what can set you back for years. I will mention that kind of math exercise several times in this book, at it is vitally important to understanding asset allocation for the twenty-first century.

"Moderately Constructive" and Other Indecipherable Comments from "Talking Heads"

As I often tell my industry colleagues, watching some of CNBC's programming is a must if you are a portfolio manager or financial advisor. That's not because the content is compelling (perhaps it is if you are a trader, though if people are broadcasting their best trading ideas simultaneously to millions of other traders, there goes your "edge," I suppose). The reason to at least keep tabs on what is being said in the TV financial media is that many of your clients watch, and some watch avidly. Thus, part of the role of any portfolio manager or financial advisor is to be prepared to separate for your investors and clients what is truly valuable information versus that which is noise pollution on the public airwaves. With that as a starting point, consider this brief discussion I heard one morning last week.

A guest told the interviewer, "We think the stock market has 10 to 15 percent more upside—we are moderately constructive there." What the heck does "moderately constructive" mean?! I have heard the last part of that phrase used by many market watchers, and it seems that it's more a way to avoid committing to an answer than providing useful information. Of course, the preponderance of questions such as "Where is the market headed?" can often be more about entertaining than informing anyway, since market results sometimes prove that forecasting is a crapshoot anyway. Importantly, evaluating the current trade-off between market risk and reward is not a crapshoot, as it allows one to consider what can happen if you are wrong and hopefully guard against it. *That* is what we do not see enough of in the financial press, in my opinion.

Congratulations!

For what, you say? For completing the portion of this book that looks back; reflects on what has happened to investors and their advisors, particularly over the past 30 years; and draws some general conclusions about the do's and don'ts of asset allocation, portfolio management, and the work of getting to where you want to be. If you made it this far, you get an "A." If you didn't, it doesn't matter what I write here because you will never see it. How's that for lenient grading?

Now, let's move on to the biggest reason you are reading this book: to figure out how to intelligently and methodically allocate assets and make investment decisions in the twenty-first century!

PART

III

INVESTING IN THE TWENTY-FIRST CENTURY

Keys to Successful Asset Allocation

THE "NEW NORMAL"

After 2008, many market commentators began to discuss something called the "new normal." The idea is that for investors, what they once knew as normal or typical market, investor, and consumer behavior had been replaced by something very different. From what I've seen from my perch so far, I cannot argue with that.

However, that does not mean that we throw in the towel. It does mean that we change the playbook, back to one that has not been used during most investors' lifetimes. The good news is that in using this new playbook, the players are faster and stronger. That is, the tools we have at our disposal to execute those plays are more plentiful. If you learn how to use them, you can survive whatever comes at us from here, including a surprise return to the old normal, should that occur at some point. Most importantly, you can do better than survive—you can thrive. That's what this book is about.

Earlier, we reviewed some of the most important issues for investors today. We then saw that Wall Street may help or hinder as you seek to address those issues. In this chapter, I provide my opinions, beliefs, and structural guidance on how an investor can greatly increase his chances of investment success in the twenty-first century.

One of the most important pieces of guidance I've ever received is that there are some things in life that we can control and some that we can't. At least once a week, something happens to remind me that this is critical to remember. If we focus less on what happens to us and more on what we can do about it, we are much better off.

In this chapter, I point out some of the most important concepts you should understand as a twenty-first-century investor. I then share my thoughts on what types of investments I believe give you the best shot at living the lifestyle you envision.

Note that I'm not going to call out a stock or market sector. I'm simply going to summarize many years of a "process of elimination" analysis about what you should focus on and what you should ignore as an investor today. I say "today" for a very important reason: as discussed earlier, there is a "conventional wisdom" that many of us grew up with as investors in the 1980s and 1990s that is fading into obscurity. If you don't recognize this, your portfolio's value may fade, too.

It will come as no surprise to you that I did not arrive at these "keys to asset allocation" overnight. I think that in order to understand how this can help you, you need a brief background on the evolution of all of this.

An Investment Philosophy Is Born

While my career in the investment industry began back in 1986, the development of what I practice today as a professional money manager started in the late 1990s. Very simply, I started to recognize what I felt were severe gaps in the traditional investment offering, and set out to find ways to fill those gaps. A prime part of the solution involved the ability to use the "short" side of the stock market. That is, to profit from market declines instead of just hoping it went up. Cash has been a good way to "hedge" portfolios, but interest rates were in a secular decline since the early 1980s and I suspected that cash would not be sufficient by itself as an alternative to stocks and bonds, particularly during periods of market stress.

After cofounding Emerald Asset Advisors in 1998, I was able to start incorporating that philosophy into an investment process. In the early years of this approach, I selected money managers for each client based on our perception of their ability to pursue the type of nontraditional, lower-volatility return pattern we desired. It did not take me long to figure out that this was an inefficient process to say the least. I started to realize that while we implemented the approach via individual accounts with outside money managers, we did not have sufficient control over the investment

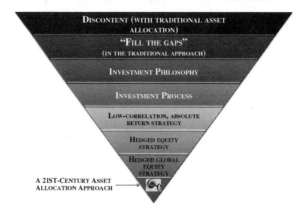

DISCONTENT (WITH TRADITIONAL ASSET ALLOCATION)

"FILL THE GAPS" (IN THE TRADITIONAL APPROACH)

INVESTMENT PHILOSOPHY

INVESTMENT PROCESS

LOW-CORRELATION, ABSOLUTE RETURN STRATEGY

HEDGED EQUITY STRATEGY

HEDGED GLOBAL EQUITY STRATEGY

A 21ST-CENTURY ASSET ALLOCATION APPROACH

Figure 6.1　The Evolution of the Asset Allocation Strategies

process and decision making. The control we did have was limited by a glut of paperwork needed to change managers each time we had a change of opinion. In summary, this was not going to be a long-term solution for our clients or ourselves. It was time to create a more fluid investment process based on this nontraditional investment philosophy I had developed (see Figure 6.1).

The Philosophy Leads to an Investment Process

I had used mutual funds in my investment practice since 1993 and, through the course of my research, realized that the majority of funds were very generic. They invested in stocks, bonds, or both, and tended to follow the market up and down. This kind of "following the herd" behavior had limited value in a long bull market, and during the 1990s, funds that tried to track a market index instead of beating it were all the rage. It seemed as if active management would never be needed again. Then came the 2000–2002 bear market, and we became convinced that traditional asset allocation strategies and buy-and-hold investing were not enough.

A major regulatory change occurred in the stock market back in 1997, and to some degree it paved the way toward the development of my investment process. It involved the extent to which investors could "short" stocks.

While some of the hedged mutual funds we use have been around since the 1970s and 1980s, it was not until 1997 that the door opened wide for this approach to be developed. What happened in 1997? The "short-short" rule was eliminated. This rule limited mutual funds' ability to sell securities they had owned for less than three months to 30 percent of their assets. The repeal of the rule allowed mutual funds to engage in short selling and other hedging techniques to a much greater degree than they could prior to 1997. This effectively was the birth of hedged mutual fund investing, and it is what prompted me to start the long research journey that ultimately led to what you are reading about in this book. You may recall that in late 2008, short selling was restricted for a brief period. Investors were prohibited from selling stocks of nearly 800 financial companies. The Securities and Exchange Commission (SEC) issued a press release on September 19, 2008, explaining this move. The release included the following:

> This decisive SEC action calls a time-out to aggressive short selling in financial institution stocks, because of the essential link between their stock price and confidence in the institution. The Commission will continue to consider measures to address short selling concerns in other publicly traded companies.

The ban was eventually lifted, and the political and business debate about the appropriateness and efficacy of the move could fill another book, so I won't take it on in much detail here. However, I have had many people ask me what I'd do if short selling were banned again, maybe even permanently. Wouldn't that greatly impact the ability to run the kind of asset allocation strategies we are discussing in this book?

What If They Ban Short-Selling Again?

Now, if short selling were banned permanently, it might fix one problem but bring up another: market integrity. Short sellers play a role in the marketplace, and regulators' job is not to artificially pump up the stock market by eliminating those rooting against it.

More importantly, if short selling were somehow restricted in a way that it would be tougher to execute strategies that include shorting, there is another way: the options market. In fact, I have made frequent use of options in my portfolio management career, particularly as a way to hedge an equity investment without committing a large cash outlay. Options allow you to take a position on a stock, exchange-traded fund (ETF), or market index (long or short), but based on the probability of that security's reaching a certain price level by a predetermined date. No, it is not the same as shorting, but there is a trade-off: While options do not function as the exact opposite of the return of the underlying security—as is the case with shorting—options allow you to pursue the same sentiment as a short sale, but with a much lower amount of capital at risk, and potentially similar or better results.

I won't go into any more detail on options here because you can get more perspective on this by going online. The bottom line is that in the unlikely event that shorting is eliminated as a strategy, options can be a very good surrogate, in my opinion. I will note that using options can be cumbersome in a "separate account" environment, and that they function more smoothly within a pooled investment vehicle such a mutual fund. Now, back to our story (of the creation of the allocation strategies).

The hedge fund industry was the new glamour investment in investors' minds by 2002. While my team and I believed that hedge funds were to be considered for some investors, we felt that there was much to be said for using mutual funds to pursue the same type of "low-correlation" return stream that hedge funds had become known for. I decided to start creating portfolios that mixed these funds, with the goal of achieving better risk-adjusted returns over time than the traditional approach. The philosophy that inspired an investment process had, over the course of a few years, led to a trio of investment portfolios. We ran these portfolios for our own clients, and the approach seemed to be working.

As we attended industry conferences and met other financial advisors, we told them what we were doing for our clients and how it was enhancing our practice. Based on their reactions, we started to realize that there was a market for what we were doing, among other advisors.

The 10 Keys to Asset Allocation

In 2005, we were contacted by the sponsor of a "mutual fund wrap" program who had heard about our efforts in this area. They asked us to make our portfolios available to advisors who used their investment manager access program, and after completing their due diligence process, we obliged. More "wrap sponsors" followed, and we had begun to make these diversified asset allocation strategies available to investors outside of our own firm, through their advisors. We also took the arduous and now ongoing step to have our investment returns scrutinized to the level of accuracy dictated by the Global Investment Performance Standards (GIPS), published by the CFA Institute.

As we continued the dialogue we had started with our financial advisor peers, we started to realize that for many of them, the most convenient delivery vehicle for them was the mutual fund. Given our long history with using funds, we decided to start a mutual fund ourselves, in 2008. Over a decade after the development of the philosophy, we entered the "public" market, effectively putting our performance on display on a daily basis.

When I look back at what I created, I think I can reduce the detail down to 10 key factors that should be part of the any asset allocation approach in the twenty-first century. They are:

1. *Be flexible in the investment process.* Investment flexibility means not limiting yourself unnecessarily in your pursuit of preservation and growth of capital. Why don't many portfolio managers use cash as a defensive measure? Why don't they use the short side of the market? Why don't they incorporate lower-volatility styles to go alongside their traditional portfolio structure? Don't ask me, ask them! Seriously, though, most mutual funds have the ability to use a wide range of strategies when unique circumstances arrive. They disclose this in their prospectus; they pay their attorneys to check it over and make sure they are protected legally, down to the letter. And then they don't use the flexibility they granted themselves!

    A good explanation for this is that those fund managers do not feel they have the requisite skill set to use these tools wisely and to the shareholders' benefit. That's okay, but if it is the case, you have to consider whether such funds are flexible enough for your tastes. Remember, this is not the 1990s anymore.

2. *Be adaptive to major changes in the economic and market environment.* This requires very little explanation. In 2008, life gave you lemons. Did your portfolio managers make lemonade? Within the limits of a mutual fund's prospectus, I feel strongly that a manager should protect your capital by all means

necessary when the markets "hit the fan." And when conditions change for the better, don't expect them to react in knee-jerk fashion. However, you don't want to see them still hunkered down, fighting the last war. As you know, you can sit in cash for an extended period of time all by yourself; you don't need a pro to do it for you. It is a constant balancing process for a money manager to be adaptive. It is not easy, and that is why professional portfolio and fund management is a skilled position. Again, some indexing-happy members of the media and index fund product providers are still content to let investors wilt in tough markets and permit the assumption to persist that professional money managers are all, as the line from the classic movie *Animal House* goes, "worthless and weak."

3. *Be opportunistic—but not aggressive.* I have seen over and over again that people automatically associate high returns with aggressive tactics. The "crash and burn" risk of investing on margin and focusing a lot of money in helter-skelter strategies often finishes second to consistent, patient, lifestyle-oriented approach thinking. It's the tortoise-hare thing applied to your wealth. The difference between aggressive investing and opportunistic investing is often the size of the move you make. For instance, putting 50 percent of your portfolio in commodities, even if it works out, is an aggressive move. Recognizing that commodities are volatile, and allocating 5 percent of your portfolio to them because you feel that market segment can spike up in the coming months, is opportunistic. Again, it may not work out, but the cost to you if it doesn't is known and controlled before the decision to buy it is made. Think about it this way: if you lost 20 percent on that 5 percent position, your overall portfolio is impacted by only 1 percent. If you lost only 6 percent on a 50 percent position, that impacts your portfolio by 3 percent.

Final exam on this subject: which of those outcomes is a result of aggressive investing, and which is an attempt to be opportunistic that did not work out, but allowed you to live to fight another day?

4. *Go beyond "style boxing."* Morningstar, the well-known securities data and analysis firm, has created many proprietary tools over the years. One of their best known is the "style box."

This grid contains nine boxes, and each box represents the type of investment (growth, value, or core—mix of growth and value) and the size of the companies involved (large, medium, or small cap). The style box spawned an entire segment of the investment industry. It literally took the concept of asset allocation and put it on the map. Morningstar even supplied the map. Style-box investing was all the rage in the investment advisory profession during the 1990s. In fact, if you look at how mutual funds and managed accounts are created today, a lot of it goes back to the producer's desire to build a product to fit an area of the style box. It is common to see a company with a single mutual fund, which did not have a clear style bias, renamed, say, the "large core portfolio." The management company would then introduce a large-cap growth portfolio and a large-cap value portfolio. Later on, they would build or acquire a small-cap fund, and perhaps a mid-cap, too. They'd keep going until they were confident that their sales force could now go out and market to advisors, armed with their own brand of box-filling products. I think that this is very 1990s thinking, and it is potentially very dangerous to you as an investor. The reason is simple: style-box investing does not reduce your risk as much as you think it does!

A very crafty money management firm I know touts their firm's flexibility in being able to invest in any stock style whenever they want. They refer to their philosophy as "unwrapping the box," which is clearly aimed at refuting the style-box mentality in today's postbubble environment. I'm right there with them. Investing for the next generation, in my opinion, is more about maintaining the highest degree of flexibility you can, not clinging to a rigid, boxy style of portfolio construction. I don't see anything in the latter approach (style box) that cannot be accomplished by the former (flexible). At the time I published my first book in 2006, I think my industry was subtly starting to pick up on this. A few years later, they are well aware of it, and thankfully are spreading the word to their clients, as part of the massive investor re-education process that is beginning to take place.

5. *Find bull markets wherever they exist, on both the long and short sides of the stock, bond, commodity, and currency markets.* This is covered

extensively throughout the book, but simply put, bad markets call for investors to pursue profits, or at least attempt to reduce losses, by investing in ways that succeed if the stock market falls. Review the grid on this subject from earlier in the book if you need a refresher on where some likely bull markets would occur in different economic environments.

6. *Aim to capture the majority of the market's ups, and a lesser portion of its downs.* I could not blame you if you responded to that sentence with a sarcastic "duh!" Of course, you want to grab more of the market's goodness and avoid most of the damage. Understand that it is easy to set such a goal, but based on the history of the professional investment management business, it's hard to achieve. Again, that is why I put such a premium on doing initial and ongoing investment research on mutual funds. That analysis is not limited to simply reviewing past performance.

   If you can capture most of the market's ups and a lesser portion when it declines, that should give you a higher probability of achieving your investment objectives than an approach that simply mimics the movement of the stock and bond markets. The research process is the differentiating factor here.

7. *Avoid the big loss.* As we hear another resounding "duh" from the audience, consider that in 2008, many investors lost 40 percent or more of their investment portfolio value. Think about what that really means. Even if you had built up your portfolio's value for decades, $2 out of every $5 you accumulated was gone! Around our firm we have a mantra that I repeat to nearly every audience I have the honor of speaking to: **don't turn a dollar into 60 cents**. That is, do whatever you can to keep your portfolio's value within a reasonable distance of where you started.

   In theory this should be the most logical advice ever given to a professional financial advisor. However, a quick look at the 2008 performance charts will show you just how often this happens. You can also look back to the 2000–early 2003 period, when similar losses occurred in the broad equity markets around the world. I am not saying that a portion of one's portfolio won't take a big hit once in a while. That cannot always be avoided.

However, in the aggregate, you just cannot afford to turn that dollar into 60 cents. In fact, for quite a large number of investors, the events of late 2007 and 2008 convinced them that they did not accurately gauge their true tolerance for market-related volatility. They thought they could stare a loss of, say, one third of their assets, and still wake up smiling on their way to retirement, or while in retirement. Many of them found out they misjudged themselves.

Since everyone's tolerance for volatility is different, that means that quantifying what the "big loss" means in dollars or percentages is an individual decision. We remind financial advisors that this is perhaps the most important and valuable part of their job today. Not only do they need to successfully measure in advance to what level that dollar can fall before major changes must be made to pacify their clients. They also must realize that if they are too far off and the client suffers a big loss, their financial planning practice may be severely impacted, as clients "vote with their feet" and choose another advisor.

This reminds me of the old line about if a tree falls in the forest and there is no one there to hear it, does it make a sound? I don't have an answer for that one, but I will say this: if an investor is paying someone for professional advice, and the client sees their dollar turn into 60 cents one year, the advisor can respond with a brilliant recovery the following year, but it won't matter. You see, even if that 60 cents was managed back to, say, 80 cents (a 33 percent gain from the 60 cent level), the clients may not be there to hear it. They may have left the advisor and moved on to another advisor, or become their own advisor. Both happened frequently in reaction to the financial disaster of 2008.

If history is any guide (and it certainly is), there will be more market shocks and more client turnover. Since this does not benefit the client or the incumbent advisor, I see the role of firms like mine and investment processes like the one I have created as a major tool in the toolbox of the investor and their advisor. We truly believe we have the potential to save you from unhappy outcomes.

To summarize, I tell audiences that other than breaking even, there are four things that can happen with an investment: It can make a little, make a lot, lose a little, or lose a lot. The first three are all acceptable in the course of a long-term investment program. The latter can be fatal.

8. *Keep losses short and shallow.* Let's make one thing clear: losses are going to happen. Losses incurred over a short period of time (days, weeks, months) come with the territory if you are a serious investor (as opposed to a trader). The idea of keeping the magnitude of such losses shallow is an extension of the example used in number 7. Think about those Dow Jones historical charts earlier in the book and also about the 60/40 exercise I presented earlier. Put them together, and think about how far ahead of the market you would be if you were able to tag along on the upside and play good defense as well. Except for manias like the 1980s and 1990s, I think you beat the market easily.

9. *Use short side of the market and cash as needed, to help play defense.* This is an extension of number 5, with the added opinion that cash can be used as a defensive "weapon," but it's not as easy as it seems. "Going to cash" is a pure timing move and should be avoided. Raising cash in moderation, in consideration of what else is in the portfolio, is a more prudent strategy.

10. *Target a minimum acceptable outcome of positive returns over any three-year period.* Determining your time horizon is an essential exercise for any investor. What takes a bigger mental adjustment for many people in our sound bite, "what have you done for me lately" world is to consider what I call an appropriate "manager evaluation" horizon. For instance, one strategy I manage has a stated objective of at least breaking even over three years, no matter how bad the investment landscape is. It also aims to deliver as high a return as is reasonable given market conditions over any three-year period. Thus, you can evaluate the investment based on a month's performance, a year's, or 18 months'. In all cases, you are not evaluating it the way the manager does, so you are clearly not on the same page. I am not saying that you don't invest in a fund that is managed for the long term when you are evaluating in the short term. Just be prepared for your expectations not to be met, as it's more likely than if you match yourself up with investments and investors who manage to a comfortable time horizon for you.

Other Key Factors to Consider in Asset Allocation

While the 10 items just listed may be the most critical to consider in allocating assets, there is much more to it. In order to round out the discussion, here are the other factors that must be considered and understood prior to embarking on an effort to establish an asset allocation structure.

What Investment Vehicle to Use?

For most of the past decade, hedge funds and hedge funds-of-funds (i.e., vehicles that invest in many other hedge funds with a firm overseeing the selection and monitoring of those funds) were a popular way for affluent investors to access the kind of investment strategies covered in this book. The events of 2008 brought to light some of the disadvantages of both types of vehicles, the main one being lack of liquidity—you can't get your money out when you want it. That important fact effectively gave hedge fund managers a time window in which they could fudge, "Ponzi," or outright steal from their investors. It became for investors and their advisors the realization of our worst nightmare—that a client's money was not really safe in some of the places it was assumed to be safe.

This is why I have always been a fan of mutual funds. Mutual funds have been around since 1924, and the only scandals concerning them were due to the actions of some unscrupulous people who gave preferential treatment to certain big clients of their funds. This occurred in the first few years of the twenty-first century, and the toll on investors when all was said and done was minimal. You can Google "mutual fund late-trading scandal" or something like that if you want to learn more. The mutual fund structure itself has been a survivor, and that should allow investors and their financial advisors to have a comfort level with them. As you know, after 2008, comfort is at a premium in the business of investing your hard-earned money.

If we learned anything from 2008's horrific events, it is this: investment strategies of varying types should be pursued. However, it is best to pursue them with a financial vehicle that is a proven, reliable holding place for those strategies. I come out of this discussion with the same conclusion I had before 2008: for most investors and their advisors, mutual funds are a great vehicle to use. ETFs are a step below but still very viable as long as they are not misused. Individual stocks are only for the truly savvy and risk-aware, and hedge funds and private equity funds are for a select few who have both the assets to participate and the awareness of the risks that go with the potential rewards of private investment vehicles.

Mutual funds have some advantages that you should be reminded of. As opposed to investing in individual stocks, a fund's assets and transaction costs are divided among all the mutual fund shareholders, which allows for cost-effective diversification. Mutual funds are available at varying minimum investment levels, but they generally tend to be very affordable for most investors to consider. Mutual funds are owned not by the fund company, but by the shareholders. That is a fact that is often misunderstood. The manager of the fund has a management contract with the fund, but the shareholders collectively are the true owners of the fund entity. Remember, mutual funds were originally created to offer investors a way to pool their assets together, in order to have a professional investor make investments on their behalf, for their "mutual" benefit.

The Investment Company Institute (ICI) has an outstanding presentation to educate investors about the basic purpose and structure of mutual funds and mutual fund investing. You can find it at this link: www.ici.org/pdf/bro_understanding_mfs_p.pdf.

A mutual fund's organizational structure contains several important parties. It is not simply a guy in a small room making trades and publishing returns. The fund's investment advisor is obligated to manage to the objectives and policies spelled out in the fund's prospectus document. The fund administrator is responsible for making sure those who provide services to the fund are in compliance with regulations. Each fund has a transfer agent to keep records of shareholder activity in the fund, ensures that transactions in the fund are completed properly, and provides standard fund documents (such as account statements and annual reports) to all shareholders.

The fund's assets are held by its custodian. The custodian maintains separate accounting of each shareholder's assets, so that everyone's specific "piece of the pie" can be identified. Finally, the fund has an independent public accountant (emphasis on the word *independent*), who certifies that the fund's financial statements are accurate.

Mutual funds are heavily regulated entities. For the investor, that regulation is very good news. The Securities and Exchange Commission (SEC) is the primary regulator, attempting to identify and eliminate any fraudulent activities, reviewing funds' required filings, and developing new regulations as needed.

The SEC's Office of Compliance Inspections and Examinations administers a nationwide examination and inspection program for mutual funds. The Office of Investor Education and Assistance addresses concerns from investors about mutual funds.

Why Not Just Use ETFs?

There is a growing segment of the investor population that thinks ETFs are a full replacement for mutual funds. I don't think they are. ETFs are a terrific invention, but segments of Wall Street seized on the opportunity to commercialize them and are in the process of overdoing it. That does not mean I don't use ETFs. I do and will continue to. But I use the "best available athlete" approach to whether an ETF or mutual fund is the right choice to participate in an investment style or theme I have decided to invest in. In some cases, there is an ETF but no mutual fund. For instance, I know of no mutual fund that invests 100 percent in gold bullion. All mutual funds dedicated entirely to the gold market invest in gold stocks. Thus, if we want pure exposure to gold bullion versus the gold stocks, we will likely use an ETF. Gold stocks tend to react to the price of gold, but can also be swung around by the vagaries of the stock market, making them an imperfect surrogate for owning the metal itself.

I believe that ETFs are another example of Wall Street's overdoing a good idea. One problem I see is that a lot of ETFs are copycats of other products. It's not so much that there are three or four ETFs to mimic the S&P 500—that can be healthy competition. It's the scores of ETF issues whose risk-reward profile does not differ significantly from the broad market. This is the same problem that exists in the mutual fund world, that there are many "closet indexers"—funds that appear to be doing something that will perform differently than an index fund with the same objective, but in reality they are managed so that they can track the market, not err too far from the market's return, and collect a hefty fee. Since most ETFs are based on index strategies, issuers have come up with a zillion ways to cut the same pie, and the absence of active management means that we have a big group of quantitative index chasers out there. My expectation is, as in the past, that many of the investors whose money flows into these ETFs will be very disappointed when they see them correlate highly to future declines in the broad stock market.

Another issue with ETFs is that too many of them trade minimal volume, well after their issuance. That is a problem. Where's the value added there? In too many cases, I don't see it. Remember, lack of liquidity is the source of many problems for investors when markets get rough. A large segment of the ETF world may succumb to this eventually.

I also see many money managers and advisors trying to simplify their investment approach by using ETFs, either strategically (buy and hold) or tactically. The problem some will have is what we refer to as *capacity constraints*. If an ETF does not trade very high volume, the investment manager will be able to buy only a modest amount, or risk having a logjam at the door when they want to leave the room (e.g., sell the position). The fact that many advisors are taking their first formalized shot at building a formal investment track record in this fashion leads me to believe that, as in the past, the masses will get it wrong. That will make for many disappointed advisors and many frustrated clients.

Hedge Funds: A Limited Solution

In case you want to see some of what I was saying about hedge funds from my first book, I will repeat it here. I think you will find that the nail was hit on the head in this case.

Notable Pros and Cons of Hedge Funds

Pros

- *Absolute return focus.* The focus on making money instead of competing with some traditional stock index is desirable.
- *Flexible investment style.* With flexibility comes opportunity, as long as the money is in capable hands.
- *Top manager talent.* Many capable hands have left other investment structures to run hedge funds. As long as they exploit their talent and don't let greed in the door, this is a good thing for hedge fund investors.

- *Well diversified.* Funds-of-funds typically diversify among as few as 5 or as many as 100 hedge funds. While the higher end of this range clearly qualifies as "de-worse-ification" and not diversification, the principal of spreading one's risk is key to hedged investing, or any other type of investing.

Cons

We refer to the "TLC" of hedge fund investing—transparency, liquidity, and cost. However, there is not much tender loving care going on when:

- *Transparency is limited.* If you don't really know what type of activities are being performed deep in the bowels of your hedge fund, lost in the shuffle of a 60-manager fund-of-funds, there is the risk I call "what you don't know *will* hurt you."
- *Liquidity is limited.* If you took the advice of your broker and put a big chunk of your assets in a fund that can only be sold every six months, you had better not need that money unexpectedly.
- *The costs are high and layered.* In "the old days" (1990s until about 2001), if the hedge fund managers in a fund-of-funds made 20 percent, and the various layers of fees were deducted, a 13 percent return might result. I think that clients who saw a consistent return of around 13 percent a year probably were not asking a lot of questions about fees. Thirteen percent is a strong return, especially compared to bond rates at the time.

As the fund-of-hedge-funds industry became more crowded, and scandals erupted here, there, and everywhere, returns on these private investment partnerships moderated. Unfortunately for hedge-fund-of-funds managers, their fee structure backfires on them when returns moderate. If the underlying hedge fund managers scrape out only, say, a gross return of 10 percent, after the pounds of flesh are taken out by the managers' fees, profit incentive fees, and the fund-of-funds' fees, the net return could be more like 5 percent. Again, when 20 percent nets you 13 percent, you don't ask a lot of questions. When 10 percent nets you 5 percent, and you are carrying all the potential baggage represented by the TLC of hedge fund investing, you *will* be asking questions. It stops being a prudent investment at that point.

Without a doubt, *the* most overlooked aspect of hedge fund investing is heavy tax burden that comes with many of them, for taxable investors. Now, I'm not a tax advisor, but I do know that you can find out how a hedge fund or fund-of-funds is taxed by reading the documents that created it.

The last hedge fund conundrum has to do with what regulatory environment you are operating in. For investors who have used stocks, bonds, mutual funds, and options, they are operating in the world of investments registered with and overseen by SEC, one of the principal regulatory bodies of my industry. Where does a hedge-fund-of-funds fit into this?

For some time, hedge funds and funds-of-funds did not have to register with the SEC. The SEC started requiring registration in February 2006. While many hedge funds found loopholes to temporarily suspend their requirement to register, most started to do so when they were required. A short time later, the registration requirement was lifted. Guess what happened next? Hedge funds started to deregister again, in large numbers. The "hot potato" among U.S. legislators and regulators on this issue aside, it seems that hedge fund managers prefer to tilt their businesses toward the less regulated, less transparent side. That's okay for them, but from what I have witnessed, investors have been much more wary of that behavior since 2008.

Of course, even if the fund-of-funds entity and the hedge funds in it are registered, the investment made by those underlying funds can be in anything. That includes, well, just about everything. In my opinion, this leaves room for many of the same abuses that have occurred in the past. The financial services industry does not always learn from its mistakes. Investors are getting wise to that.

So, the bottom line for me: hedge funds may be considered for a select group of "big boys and girls"—those very well-heeled clients who can view hedge fund investing as a lark, and as something whose limited liquidity is worthy of a modest portion of their portfolio, but nothing more. And for that lack of liquidity, they should demand consistently superior returns from their managers and a level of transparency sufficient for a "prudent person" to conclude that the money is safe-kept and the investment reporting from the fund is accurate and real. Otherwise, why bother? The thrill and exclusivity of the hedge fund business was a big attraction to investors many years ago. I think the bloom is surely off that rose after 2008. But, lest you think the public has caught on, how about this fact: In January 2009, an ETF that tracks a hedge fund index, issued by Deutsche Bank, made its debut in London. By mid-December of that same year, it had crossed $1 billion in assets, according to a press release from that firm. The fund was billed as a "liquid and transparent form of access for investors who want exposure to the hedge fund market." Old habits die hard, and old wounds sometimes disappear from the memory once they have healed. Do investors want hedge fund "replication," or do they want the benefits of hedged investing but with some thought and active management behind it? As I represent the latter camp, you know where I stand.

What Holding Period/Time Horizon to Target?

With many holdings in all three of my strategies, I expect to hold them at some level over many, many years, but the position size will be adjusted as a medium-term risk measure. By contrast, the hedge positions are used primarily as a way to try to make money on short- to medium-term declines in areas of the market that are similar in content to our holdings. The goal is to profit from the short positions. However, as a fallback, they may act as a hedge against the existing portfolio, hopefully allowing you to hold the core positions longer without experiencing all of the downs, and promoting long-term capital gains over short-term gains.

While each of my strategies is broadly diversified, they are effectively two portfolios in one:

1. The core "long" portfolio.
2. A temporary short position (purchased by buying an ETF or mutual fund that shorts). This short position is not required at all times. It is used at our discretion, as we feel it is needed.

Our primary goal is to make money on the shorts in the shorter time frame we own them, and make money on the core long positions over the longer time that we own those. Of course, we may not always achieve that objective, but that's what we are aiming for.

"Target-Date" Funds: Way Off Target!

Target-date funds are sold to investors as an all-in-one investment portfolio in that they allocate among the broad stock and bond markets. They are designed to adjust the allocation based on how many years remain until the investor's target retirement date. This is not necessarily the date when the investor will stop working, but it is the date to which the fund is managed. In other words, the target dates are set with the masses in mind, and the investor may choose a fund that is aiming to reach its objective at a point close to where they expect the use the money.

I believe that for many investors in their preretirement years, target-date funds are not just a bad idea but a misleading one. As I said earlier, target-date funds allocate money among the broad stock and bond markets. But in doing so, they are setting themselves up for failure in two ways. First, by limiting Target Date Fund investments to traditional stock and bond strategies, the investor has what I would call "correlation risk"—when stocks fall, they tend to fall as a group. That means that the investor, who expects their target-date fund's stock portfolio to fall by a modest amount owing to their diversification among small-cap, large-cap, growth, value, and international stocks, ends up disappointed. They are disappointed because the expected benefit of diversification does not accrue to them— when markets fall hard, all major categories of stocks fall together. This is what broke so many hearts and so many retirement dreams in 2008 and early 2009. I think that target-date funds provided a false sense of security then, and I have seen no evidence to be any more optimistic now.

In 2008, bonds were a savior to target-date funds, as U.S. Treasury securities surged in value when investors fled to their perceived safety. But that ship may have sailed, and the next stock market decline may not offer a hiding place in high-quality bonds like Treasuries. Why not? Because they are increasingly viewed as not being of high quality anymore! The debt being racked up by the U.S. and many non-U.S. governments has called the stability of U.S. interest rates into question. That is not to say that I think the U.S. government will default on its debt. I just believe they will have to pay much higher rates to borrowers to keep the country functioning. As that happens, rates go up and bond prices go down. Combine that with a stock market that, while possibly in long-term recovery mode, will not likely advance in a smooth path. The bottom line: a traditional mix of stocks, bonds, and even cash will lead many target-date fund investors to look back and feel they were misled by the promise of a "managed" path to retirement.

In order to remedy this, target-date funds must look beyond traditional investment styles. They should be willing to incorporate, in a thoughtful and flexible manner, the ability to profit from market declines through shorting and other hedging approaches. They should also allow longer-dated target-date funds to pursue investments in areas that have the potential for long-term outsized returns compared to traditional equities, though they may be more volatile along the way. Some areas of the emerging markets as well initiatives such as clean energy and global infrastructure are examples of such open-minded thinking that is not presently accounted for in most target-date offerings.

The other misleading feature is the so-called "glide path." As a fund gets closer and closer to its target date, it automatically becomes more conservative, with more of the assets going to bonds and away from stocks. This automatic shift in assets could end up being the worst-case move for investors. What if you bought a target-date fund that targets a 2015 retirement date, and you bought it back in 2000. As of early 2010 your total return net of taxes was probably somewhere around zero, give or take a few percent. Why? Because your fund allocated heavily to stocks when you bought it in 2000—right as the market peaked. Now that you are within a handful of years to retirement in 2015, your glide path will dictate that you accelerate the shift out of stocks and bulk up on bonds instead—at a point where bond rates were at historic lows, so upside was limited for you there. Talk about an "off-target" investment plan!

The criteria I would advise an investor to use when evaluating asset allocation strategies are not met by any target-date funds on the market, at least not as of the writing of this book. The key thing investors should insist on when pursuing a plan to put their retirement investment savings plan on "auto-pilot" is the ability to adapt to changes in the broad financial market environment. I am not talking about trading, but about longer-term cyclical and secular changes in the stock and bond markets. The stock and bond markets ebb and flow over time, and to simply determine today what asset allocation changes you will make many years from now (which is what a glide path does) seems ludicrous to me. In retirement investing, like life itself, hurdles and surprises come at you, and you have to adapt. Target-date funds do not prepare investors for that unfortunate reality.

Allocation Funds: A Better Solution for Preretirees

While I dislike target-date funds, the fact remains that for many investors, allocation funds, in which an investor gets a wider "set it and forget it" portion of their portfolio, are a good way to prevent self-inflicted investment wounds. Fortunately, there are less complicated solutions. There are several capable mutual funds that allocate among different traditional and nontraditional asset classes. Some are managed by a single firm using multiple styles, and others take a "multimanager" approach, in which the fund manager allocates among several money management firms, each with its own specific style. The fund manager's job is to find and maintain a mix of managers and styles that allows the fund to pursue its stated objectives. Again, hedging is not common here, but it's a lot more common than in the target-date fund universe. For the strategies and mutual funds I manage, this is a central part of my responsibility: putting the asset allocation puzzle together and adjusting when needed.

By using a more flexibly managed approach for their retirement portfolio, people approaching retirement are better off. Why? The glide path problem is largely negated, as the allocation fund manager is charged with balancing risk and return at all times. Allocation funds don't specifically target a retirement date, but compared to target-date funds, I firmly believe they give you a far better chance to get there, and the possibility of a much smoother ride along the way.

Note that most target-date funds and many allocation funds are run by money management firms with massive assets, massive distribution muscle, and massive advertising budgets. But it would be a massive mistake for an investor to simply choose a retirement-oriented fund based on the assumed comfort that goes with size. On Wall Street, we have seen over and over the past few years that the bigger they are, the harder they fall.

The True Cost of Investing

Here is my conclusion regarding the cost of investing, as it applies to mutual funds (though it is not too different when discussing other types of investments): **you get what you pay for!**

One of our biggest pet peeves is the attitude the investment public has taken toward mutual fund expense ratios. I have written about this subject many times in the *GreenThought$* newsletter issues, and have been interviewed on it in the national media. The conventional wisdom for many years was that you had to be an idiot to invest in mutual funds that did not have the lowest or near the lowest expense ratios in their peer groups. Then, a fellow named D. Bruce Johnsen, a law professor at George Mason University in Virginia, came along, with a 2009 study called *Myths about Mutual Fund Fees: Economic Insights on* Jones v. Harris. As reported in an article on DailyFinance.com, which I was also interviewed for shortly after the study came out, he summarized his conclusions as follows:

> Lower advisory fees don't necessarily benefit investors. Don't believe the bad press about high advisory fees. It's a misconception that fund fees necessarily reduce investor returns dollar for dollar, and that lower fees therefore benefit investors.

To summarize my own rationale for owning mutual funds that don't have the lowest expense ratios, and having to argue this point with many in my industry:

- Beginning with the mega-bull market in the 1990s, members of the financial services industry (mostly larger firms, but more recently ETF providers, too) convinced investors that lower fund expenses for management and administration were synonymous with better investment results.
- The investing public bought that advice and sunk hoards of cash into index funds. Some thought it was "safer" to do that, since index funds have been hailed as a "smart" investment by so many "experts."
- This advice has merit in parts of the investment world, but in our opinion, it is one of the many oversimplified, mass-produced "conventional wisdoms" of the industry. In much of the mutual fund world, you get what you pay for.
- The fact is, the cost of investing in a mutual fund has many parts, namely:
    - *The expense ratio* (which covers management and operational expenses, and in some cases, a so-called 12b-1 distribution fee)
    - *The tax impact of an investment in the fund.* Over time, this may take the form of dividend income and/or capital gains. If

the fund manager does a good job of making money while minimizing taxes along the way, the cost of taxes to a taxable investor in a mutual fund is reduced. This "cost" to the investor can be much higher over time than the cost paid via the expense ratio. In our opinion, a more conscientious manager, who is motivated to be aware of the tax impact and tries to reduce it, has the potential to more than make up for any fee differential versus an index fund, over time.

- *Trading and other costs.* These are not part of the expense ratio. You have to look at a fund's "statement of additional information" to find these disclosed. If you are a very cost-sensitive investor or advisor, it makes sense to do this. The information is typically found on the fund's website or certainly by contacting the fund company.

- *The cost of poor performance.* Yes, performance actually matters in the fund business—it's not all about costs; it's about long-term return net of all costs. That is what the investor has to spend on their lifestyle. Yet it seems to me that over the past decade, many investors (and even some financial advisors) have had a difficult time reeducating themselves about the "performance vs. cost" relationship. When they do get around to it, they will find that poor performance, especially in down markets, is by far the highest cost of investing. Once they acknowledge that, the nickel-and-dime worries over expense ratios, and the automatic use of ETFs instead of mutual funds just to save a few dollars a year on cost (but maybe not in total performance) is a lot of wasted time. What they should be doing is finding an effective asset mix, and if it's not the lowest-cost provider to them, so be it.

Think about it: if you invest in a fund that, by design, is highly correlated to the movement of the stock market, guess what—in a down market, you can lose a lot of money! Does it make you feel better that you didn't pay much for the experience? The old adage that the stock market solves all investors' problems over a long period of time has been debunked. To me, the cost-of-investing discussion goes hand in hand with that.

"Getting what you pay for" often means that those who look at mutual fund investing as a research-driven process and not as a commoditized exercise (i.e., they are all the same, so just find the cheapest expense ratio) have a better chance of weathering investment storms. Given the possibility of a volatile environment for stocks *and* bonds over the next decade, it seems to me that a re-education of investors about the cost of investing and the risks of oversimplifying the cost discussion is imperative!

Portfolio Turnover: Far More Irrelevant Than "Experts" Would Have You Believe

Turnover is basically how much trading activity you have within a period of time. It is usually expressed as an annual figure. Some will argue that the more a mutual fund manager trades, the more tax-inefficient the fund will be. That is, more trading implies a higher effective tax rate on the gains you make. I think that is one of the most oversimplified and inaccurate "conventional wisdoms" in my industry.

Here is what makes me think that. First, some of the trading may be done specifically to reduce the annual tax burden to the fund's shareholders. For instance, if I own a fund or ETF whose price has declined, and there is a very similar security available, I may "swap" one for the other. As a result, the portfolio gets a loss on the sale for tax purposes, yet the portfolio is effectively unchanged. The new security is expected to perform similarly to the old security, so you have effectively garnered a "free" tax loss. That can be offset against taxable gains at some point, to negate the tax that a taxable investor would have to pay on some investment in the future. That is, the "tax loss" has a positive value to the portfolio.

Consider a strategy such as the ones I am outlining in this book. Tax swapping is a normal course of business for me, but it does mean that trades will be made that would not otherwise be performed if I didn't care about after-tax return. Ask yourself if that extra turnover is in your best interests. You bet your after-tax return it is!

Another reason to avoid getting hung up on trading turnover deals is the nature of the activity. If a mutual fund buys and sells often, and as a result replaces every security in the fund at least once every 12 months, no long-term capital gains will result. Since short-term capital gains rates are higher than long-term rates, the incentive for a taxable investor to capture as many gains of the long-term variety as possible is ignored by such a fund manager. But with good research, you know that going in.

Now, consider this: Your mutual fund manager runs what they consider to be two portfolios in one. The first is a group of holdings that the manager expects to own for over a year and probably much longer. If successful, these will be sold for long-term capital gains at some point. The other group of holdings is shorter term in nature. In other words, this second group of holdings is less strategic and more "tactical." That means that to the extent that the manager's tactical work pays off, short-term gains will be generated. Any tax swapping or losing trades will offset those short-term gains for tax purposes.

What results is a portfolio that emphasizes long-term capital gains, but whose trading turnover is largely concentrated in the second group of trades. Statistically, the turnover of the fund will be higher, but there is still ample opportunity to achieve very high "tax efficiency," where taxable investors pay only a small amount of capital gains each year. So, drawing conclusions about tax efficiency of a mutual fund or other investment vehicle based solely on trading turnover is shortsighted and can cause you to bypass some very good potential investments.

Diversification and "De-Worse-ification"

Another basic tenet that has formulated my thinking about the use of hybrids is that traditional asset allocation has many flaws. Too many asset classes tend to look like each other over time. Since we don't know in advance whether small-cap value, international growth, or something else will perform the best in the next decade, we must ask, "Why bother trying?" When I realized that there were few good answers to this question, I expanded my work on hybrid investing.

My conclusion: diversifying stocks with other stocks does not always add value to the investment process. Therefore, many investors need to look beyond traditional stock investment styles to fill their portfolio.

When to Say Bye to Your Buy (Sell Discipline)

As with any portfolio management situation, one of the critical elements of success is having a sell discipline. In fact, not having a good one is the single biggest cause of investor losses in down markets.

So, how do we decide when to exit a position in a hybrid account? There are a few guidelines I follow. The discipline for the other strategies described in future chapters is similar.

- *The price objective is achieved.* When we buy any investment for a client, we feel an obligation to know at what point we will "bail out" on both the upside and downside. This may be based on a combination of the nature of the investment and the client's individual risk tolerance. Either way, if we decide that, say, a 10 percent loss in an individual investment is the maximum pain we are willing to allow, we have to stick to it.

- *Economic/market changes.* As with any investment in a traditional style such as large-cap stocks or muni bonds, changes in the market or economic environment can prompt us to make adjustments in a hybrid portfolio. However, it is important to understand that these adjustments are a response to long-term changes, not today's latest economic headline. Nothing should be more frustrating to you as an investor than to think that someone is flipping around your hard-earned wealth based on the latest inflation report, jobs report, or economic growth estimate. But if, for instance, interest rates gradually rise for over a year, for the first time in over two decades, that might be something to react to and reposition the portfolio.

  For instance, we, along with the rest of our industry, were looking for ways to enhance clients' yields when money market rates dropped below 1 percent in 2004. Two years later, money rates were pushing 4 percent, so the need to get creative in boosting yields on cash was greatly reduced. But this also had implications for the high-yield bond market. While rates on the safest bonds rose quite a bit, rates on lower-quality, "high-yield" bonds did not rise as rapidly. This created what we call a narrowing of bond "spreads." Translated to English, when money markets were at 1 percent and high-yield bonds were at 7 percent, the latter looked good. When money markets hit close to 4 percent and high yields were at only 8 percent, high yield looked less attractive than before. What does all this mean? We watch closely to see if our exposure to high-yield bonds in the hybrid portfolios should be reduced.

- *Manager changes at a fund.* If a manager leaves, we have to ask ourselves what impact this will have on the ability of a fund to perform in the manner we have been accustomed to. If the manager was part of a strong team, their departure is no big deal. If the whole team leaves, it *is* a big deal. If the fund is run in a manner that is more mechanical than intuitive on the part of the managers, that would argue for more patience in making a decision to sell the fund. Bottom line: in the majority of cases, the people who created the track record of the fund are more important than the fund company. If they leave, the record of the fund effectively leaves with them.

- *The fund firm becomes too institutionalized.* This is something that in my opinion has received insufficient attention in my industry. Different money management firms handle success very differently. There are companies that can grow from managing $250 million to $50 billion in less than a decade, yet maintain the level of experience the client receives. In other cases, cracks in the armor appear as assets grow. As an advisor researching these firms, my team and I have to look for signs that things are not run as they were when the firm was a mere mortal, before it became a superhuman, bureaucratic goliath with national ad campaigns, a well-known spokesperson, and so on.

- *Our investment thesis is wrong—yes, it happens.* I could write a second book about all of the times I've been wrong about how an investment theme or idea eventually played out. But by acting quickly to limit losses in most of these situations, those mistakes had a low impact on the portfolio's return and no impact on the client's ability to achieve their desired lifestyle. Yes, it bears repeating once again—investing is about getting what you want out of life. It's not a competition with yourself or your friends about how much you can accumulate, and it's not about finding what worked in the past for other people and simply mimicking it. If you believe this, then it follows that large losses are the easiest way to screw up an otherwise profitable experience. Admitting that your expectations were not accurate and doing something about it is the best thing you can do for your portfolio. You advisor should know this, too.

There are other possible reasons to sell a mutual fund holding. These include a change in the fund's objective or process,

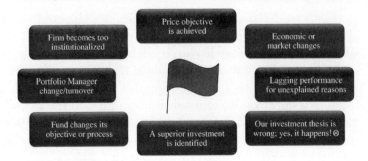

Figure 6.2   Sell Discipline

consistently lagging performance for unexplained reasons, tax-related concerns, or in cases where a superior investment has been identified (see Figure 6.2).

Volatility: How To Make It Your Friend Instead of Your Enemy

Every investing strategy has its own basic assumptions relating to risk and return. In analyzing risk, I attempt to take a realistic approach. I attempt to make a clear distinction between risk and volatility. We reviewed the idea of combating volatility earlier in the book, and now we'll apply it to hybrid investing.

If you ask most people what their greatest financial fear is, "needing money to pay for something and not having it" is probably it. That is what we call *risk*. It is permanent erosion of capital, as opposed to the wax and wane of the markets. This is something that is personal to every investor. Many experts define volatility to be the amount by which a portfolio or security will fluctuate, particularly over periods of time less than two years. This is what most clients likely mean when they talk about risk in their portfolio.

Nine Keys to Portfolio Risk Management

Why obsess about risk avoidance when you can instead manage risk intelligently? This is the question that many investors do not ever ask themselves because they cannot get beyond the basic emotion of fear. It's as if every market decline or discouraging news story about Wall Street brings on the "fight-or-flight" response—and fly away they do!

If you are truly in it for the long term, there are ways to manage risk along the way. As I pointed out earlier, "managing risk" is really "navigating through market volatility," as markets seem to always get most volatile when prices are falling, not rising.

In 2009, a financial advisor posed a very good question to me. He asked, "How do you position your portfolio to protect against the possibility of another 30 percent fall in the stock market?" While the answer is subject to the specific attitude of the investor toward risk, there are some key components that apply to all investors.

These are very much the hallmark of the investment strategies I have designed, which we will cover later in the book. When combined with the "keys to asset allocation" I present later on, you have the crux of the message about allocating assets in the twenty-first century.

In particular, these can benefit those who misjudged their own level of risk tolerance during 2008. Since I am telling you loud and clear in this book that volatility is a part of stock market investing as well as bond investing (so get used to it), it behooves you to take these keys to portfolio risk management to heart.

- *Understand market history thoroughly, so that you know what has happened before.* History doesn't always repeat itself, but it often rhymes. Many advisors and investors think of 2008 as a historical anomaly, but in fact that kind of market drop has happened many times in history. They just have not seen it in their careers or during their time as investors. Managing expectations (your client's and your own) is critical.
- *Give up the addiction to "style boxes."* This way of thinking was perfect for a runaway bull market. There is no such thing in sight now, and may not be for a long time.
- *Realize that, in our opinion, the theory much of our industry hangs their hat on is largely "bunk."* Even Gary Brinson, lead author of the famous "92 percent of your return is from asset allocation" study in 1980 has stated repeatedly that he and his colleagues never intended for it to be used as a marketing pitch by Wall Street advisors. I think we should listen to him.

  The study also focused on a small number of pension funds and did not take into account the tools advisors have at their disposal today. Pensions don't pay taxes, but individual investors do. All of that makes the study interesting, but by no means should it be the asset allocator's bible. Look how much damage bullet points two and three have caused to the psyche of the advisory business and the public these past two years! It is too bad, but there will be more periods like last autumn and winter. Do not for a minute think that strategies that failed then will succeed next time. They most likely won't.

- *Seek to minimize overlap within portfolio holdings.* Many negative surprises come from not knowing what you own in detail. See the advisor who realized that there were four large-cap value funds in the client's portfolio, and was shocked and amazed when they all fell 40 percent.

- *Err on the side of caution.* Yogi Berra said, "When you see the fork in the road, take it." We say, **"when you see the fork in the road, take the less risky route."** In other words, when faced with the choice of taking more risk to get more return versus the opposite, and it's a close call, avoid the extra risk. That includes raising cash, perhaps in significant amounts, when markets get more unpredictable than usual. A very high VIX (a stock market volatility indicator) is a better indicator that the market is unpredictable than a market that keeps falling. Falling markets at least give you something to analyze; highly volatile markets often make traditional analytical tools less useful, and that in itself is a reason to hold more cash than normal. Note that we did not say "go to cash," which we feel is akin to speculation and gambling, both of which are foreign to this writer/investor.

- *Treat each position as its own contributor to the "greater good," that is, the entire portfolio's return.* **Measure risk on each decision you make.** For instance, when we take a tactical position, we decide first how much of the portfolio it should occupy, then place a stop order. The stop order depends on our sizing up of each position's risk-reward trade-off. For instance, we may buy a 5 percent position in an ETF and place a stop order 5 percent below the purchase price. That means if we are sold out at our stop price, the entire fund will be negatively impacted by 5 percent × 5 percent = 25 bps. That's a small price to pay for tactical upside that we think is more likely to happen than not.

Now, apply that same thinking to each position, except since our core positions are usually in open-end funds, there are no stop orders. We don't need them anyway, since the expected holding period of these securities for us is several months to several years. Bottom line: your portfolio is nothing more than a thought-out collection of pieces of risk and reward and should be managed as such to make the total portfolio perform.

- *Realize that technical analysis may save your portfolio from disaster, so incorporate it into your decision making.* We often decide we are going to buy something, but also decide to hold off doing so until the technical readings on that security give us a chance to buy in at a price that is technically undervalued, or at least not overvalued. That's what technical indicators may tell you, assuming you know how to use them.

I am a huge fan of charting or "technical analysis." Once considered voodoo by many in the industry, I strongly believe that there is definitely something to be said for watching human psychology and emotions play out on my computer screen. I have found that the charts show what fundamental analysis often doesn't: what price for a security is "high" and what is "low." This is based on tracking trends in prices and trading volume. This is not a statement against fundamental financial analysis. I believe the two go hand in hand.

Technical indicators have probably had the biggest influence in my process of finalizing our decisions to buy or sell individual funds. At all times, I try to keep a "real-world" perspective as to what is going on and the impact on our clients' portfolios. To this end, I often liken the approach we take to what an NFL team's schedule is like. Each week during the season, the team prepares for its opponent. This is similar to the research process any market participant uses to determine what portfolio actions to take. For the football team, the week's preparations are important, but winning and losing occurs only on Sunday—game day.

To the portfolio strategist (me), technical analysis gives us a very good idea of what is likely to happen going forward, or least what the probability of success is. The charts are "Sunday" because regardless of what pundits say on television, and brokerage firms say in their published commentary, the only thing that ultimately determines whether money is made or lost are the changes in security prices in the markets. This is why we back up every fundamental decision with technical analysis. The charts show a picture of what is happening on the field on Sunday. The research you read or the news reports you hear is merely the equivalent of training camp.

- *Simplify your objectives into real-life goals.* Understand that relative return is considered okay for a while, but at some point you need to produce true positive returns. That pursuit is made much easier if you do a good job taking into account the following bullet point.
- *Most important: realize that when you suffer a large loss, the math works against you in a horrible way.* For instance, if you lose 50 percent, you need a 100 percent return to get back to even. If you lose even 20 percent, it takes a 25 percent return to get back to where you started. That's only a fourth of the up-move the 50 percent loser needs to repair the damage. As we say, losses are acceptable, as long as they are "short (term in nature) and shallow (in magnitude)."

You can't stop bad events from happening in the markets, but you *can* control how you prepare and react to them.

When I am asked why, for instance, news on rising inflation is greeted with rising stock prices one day and falling prices a few weeks later, I often find that a look at the chart tells the story. No event actually moves stock prices. It is market participants' *reaction* to the news that does it. Furthermore, it is often the case that the buyers or sellers of a security, sector, or the market overall get exhausted. Everyone who wants to buy has bought, and now the sellers are taking over. Or the reverse occurs. The charts tell this story the best because it is a habit of people to do the same things over and over again, including the mistakes they make. In fact, one entire philosophy of investing, the "contrarian" approach, is in its simplest form capitalizing on the mistakes of shortsighted investors. People panic sell securities of good companies along with bad ones, and contrarians wait for the sellers to get exhausted. Then they buy in.

Of course, buying and selling pressure as depicted on the charts is one way to explain all of this. The other is that the technical analysts are poking their voodoo dolls! Which one makes more sense to you?

While technical analysis has a psychological component to it, we also pay close attention to traditional sentiment indicators. In particular, we have observed that many well-known indicators are counterintuitive. A common example is the variety of investor and market advisor sentiment indicators that consistently show participants to be most bullish right before declines and most bearish at the bottom. A very wise person once said that the markets wring out the maximum amount of pain. As we have seen this proven time and again, we try to look ahead to what is likely to happen next and not get too caught up in what just happened.

Technical analysis is often our most reliable indicator as to our probability of success, but fundamental and quantitative analysis may tell us that a move we are about to make "looks" right. However, I may find that in looking at the chart, the fund we want to buy is overbought, oversold, or somewhere in the middle. I may still decide to buy something that is not at an ideal purchase price, but the allocation will likely be lower than if I felt the current price was more attractive. It is a constant trade-off between allocating to reduce volatility and market correlation and trying to buy what individual funds look most attractive at any point in time.

Five Ways to Whip Inflation Now (or Whenever It Arrives)

You read earlier about the eventual threat to investors that would be brought on by a revival of inflation. For most investors, this is a foregone conclusion but for the timing of it. Make no mistake about it, when it happens, it is likely to be a secular event. That is, the inflation era will be several years in length; it won't just come and go. It took a long time to leverage up the economy, and it will take a long time to reverse that damage. One very likely outcome at some point is rising prices of nearly everything we spend money on.

In late 2009, I received a question from an advisor that entrusts some of his clients' money to us. It was a question that should be on all investors' minds, but he asked, so he gets the credit. He goes by the nickname "Joey Grapes," owing to his enthusiasm for wine. Joey Grapes simply asked how I would position the fund during an inflationary period. Here is what I told him in response:

One thing we try not to do, as opposed to many of our peers in the investment management business, is make generalizations. For instance, we have been "expecting" inflation in the United States for some time, but it is certainly not showing up in the numbers. Just as this market cycle (down and up) since late 2007 has been atypical of "traditional" market cycles, we should not be surprised if the first inflation cycle we see in nearly 30 years, when it arrives, does not follow the expected script.

Understand that while the impact of inflation on their lifestyles is what consumers fear, it is not what investment managers should be concerned with. Instead, we are focused on inflation **expectations**, since when inflation actually arrives, some of the opportunity to take advantage of it for your investors has already slipped away. Owning funds that short both U.S. Treasuries and high-yield bonds is one way to pursue this. Gold is another, since it is looked at by many as an alternative to the world's hard currencies. In other words, when the U.S. dollar, yen, euro, and other currencies suffer from inflation in their underlying economies, their currencies are sort of "juiced." That bogs down their potential for profits, if it is suspected that such inflation can negatively impact their economy's growth. Gold has historically been a useful alternative to that.

Other ways to fight the inflation fear factor is to use Treasury inflation-protected securities (TIPS). We have not done so yet, but that is exactly what they are built for. That said, what if we feel the impact of inflation more than the government's Consumer Price Index (CPI) statistic implies. This has been the case many times. The CPI is a flawed indicator of price pressures, so again, each specific market environment demands a unique strategy.

Another decision we must make is whether stocks will be a good inflation fighter. At times, inflation is good for the stock market, as it increases the nominal value of whatever goods are sold in the economy. That may also help attract asset flow from foreign economies.

Sometimes the threat of inflation is bad news for the stock market. That has a lot to do with world investors' opinion on the overall state of our economy. For instance, despite the rise in our domestic stock market since March, the U.S. dollar suffered a large decline in 2009. To many, that looked like the rest of the world expressing their disapproval over policy in Washington (on both sides of the aisle) and the fear of a secular decline in the success of our economy. They may be looking ahead to a period of "stagflation"—not to be confused with a "stagioni" (a pizza topped with olives, mushrooms, artichoke hearts, and ham—that as well as stagflation can upset your stomach).

If that concern continues, we might consider a wager against the U.S. dollar as a way to profit from a perception of U.S. weakness whose root cause is the bubbling up of—you guessed it—inflation.

Similarly, inflation is not just a U.S. issue. We attempt to observe the threat of inflation pressures around the world. In particular, there is a strong correlation between international bond rates and inflation, at least when inflation is contained. In other words, global bond investors want to buy bonds in currencies that are strong, and sometimes the presence of moderate inflation (say, 3 to 5 percent) is viewed as a positive. We have not often treaded in global bonds, but that is certainly a possibility in the future. That would be a decision based on a combination of the aforementioned relationships between currencies, as well as inflation expectations around the world. This is where we, as a fund-of-funds manager, defer to the expertise of the underlying mutual fund managers we know. That includes those who invest in medium- to long-term bonds around the world, as well as funds that invest in short-term bonds across the globe (the equivalent of what the U.S. government issues as T-bills) to access the currency's appreciation as well as the income from short-term rates in those countries.

All of these are ways to potentially react to investment concerns either due to or derived from inflation expectations. Importantly, as with any move we make in any portfolio, we view positions taken to exploit or hedge inflation as a risk-reward assessment within the overall portfolio, not a decision made in isolation.

To summarize: inflation, like so many other issues to investors, is more of a hurdle than a problem. We can afford to view it that way because of the flexible strategies we manage, and our ability and willingness to adapt to major changes in market conditions. We feel badly for those portfolio managers whose styles constrain them so that they are forced publicly to talk up or talk down inflation to cover for their more restricted investment mandates. Okay, we don't really feel that badly for them.

Game Time! Meet the Portfolio Strategies

Now that we have reviewed the essentials for a twenty-first-century approach to asset allocation, let's put that game plan into action. The next three chapters each discuss a different asset allocation strategy I created, have used, and have audited performance figures on. Each is very different in intent and style from the other two, but they have some important common characteristics. That is why this chapter is an essential prerequisite for Chapters 7, 8, and 9. With the scene now set, let's take all we have learned about my investment philosophy, investment approach, and asset allocation parameters, and educate you about the three different portfolios that personify everything you have learned in this book so far.

The three strategies can be briefly summarized as follows:

1. **Hybrid** is a strategy that pursues long-term preservation and growth of capital over a one- to three-year period by investing in a combination of investment styles expected to exhibit low correlation to the broad stock and bond markets. Examples include long-short, market-neutral, arbitrage, high-yield bonds, and convertible bonds, among others. The key to the strategy is to carefully select and blend a group of active fund managers whose economic return drivers may differ and who tend to exhibit low correlation to one another. The goal is to create a relatively smooth return stream compared to investing only in the broad stock market.
2. **Concentrated equity** is a strategy that pursues long-term preservation and growth of capital over a three- to five-year period by investing in a group of equity money managers (through their mutual funds) who run concentrated portfolios. I define that as a manager owning 30 stocks or less. Some exceptions are made, particularly for small-cap managers, but the exceptions are modest in magnitude.
3. **Global cycle** is a strategy that pursues long-term growth and preservation of capital over a 5- to 10-year period by investing

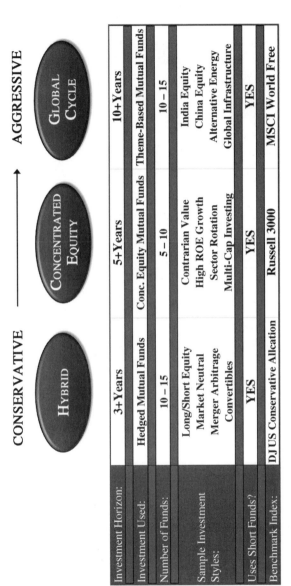

Figure 6.3   Three Separate Asset Allocation Strategies

CONSERVATIVE ⟶ AGGRESSIVE

	HYBRID	CONCENTRATED EQUITY	GLOBAL CYCLE
Investment Horizon:	3+Years	5+Years	10+Years
Investment Used:	Hedged Mutual Funds	Conc. Equity Mutual Funds	Theme-Based Mutual Funds
Number of Funds:	10 – 15	5 – 10	10 – 15
Sample Investment Styles:	Long/Short Equity Market Neutral Merger Arbitrage Convertibles	Contrarian Value High ROE Growth Sector Rotation Multi-Cap Investing	India Equity China Equity Alternative Energy Global Infrastructure
Uses Short Funds?	YES	YES	YES
Benchmark Index:	DJ US Conservative Allcation	Russell 3000	MSCI World Free

in a mix of funds that target global, secular business themes. Past examples include China, India, global infrastructure, and alternative energy, among others (see Figure 6.3).

We'll now head to Chapter 7, which covers hybrid investing, and then move on to Chapters 8 and 9, which describe concentrated equity and global cycle.

CHAPTER 7

Hybrid Investing

THE RATIONALE FOR HYBRID INVESTING

When investing the wealth you have worked so hard to achieve, you have many choices. It can be quite confusing. With all of the investment strategies out there, from the most simplistic to the utterly complex, why am I such a believer in the approach I call "hybrid investing"?

During the course of over two decades in the investment advisory business, I have had the privilege of learning about many different investment strategies. One conclusion I've reached is that there is something for everyone. The problem is that by the time many people find out what fits their investment "comfort zone," one of the following has occurred:

- They have lost a lot of money.
- They have not made enough money.
- They experienced something they didn't expect from the investment.

Very often, it is a lack of flexibility in the investment approach that caused this comfort zone to be disrupted. My hope in managing these strategies is that the investor has an easier time staying in their risk-reward "comfort zone."

As with any task in business, you have to know what outcome you seek before you can figure out how to work your way toward that outcome. Up until now this book has set the background, defined the objectives, and identified the hurdles you are likely to face on the way there. From here on, we get more "granular" as I describe the three different investment asset allocation strategies I have created and used for the benefit of investors and their advisors for several years. The philosophy that became an investment process led to this.

We start with the idea that if you can grow your assets in as consistent a path as possible, given market forces, everyone is happy. The investor is happy (as long as they keep their greed in check), and if they have a financial advisor, that advisor is happy, too. The advisor wants happy clients so they can focus their time on productive activities instead of crisis management (which is how many of them spent all of 2008). The advisor also wants some predictability in their business revenue. Investment returns that suddenly cut the value of a client's portfolio in half add tremendous uncertainty.

I seek out investment strategies and products that share this view, or that can be combined with others to pursue consistently positive returns with low correlation to the stock and bond markets. The first of three of these I will introduce to you is the first one I created. It is called "hybrid" and my formal track record in managing it goes back to late 2002.

The idea of consistent returns is a relative term. That is, hybrid is designed to be the most consistent of the three strategies I have created, and the implication of that is you give up some potential upside, at least in the short term. The majority of investors I meet are okay with that trade-off for at least part of their portfolio.

I also try very hard to shrink the range of possible outcomes for the portfolio. That is, I don't want the hybrid portfolios to have wild swings in their returns. While the stock market tends to gyrate between returns of 20 to 50 percent in either direction, we expect much smaller swings. This variation in returns among the best, worst, and average periods for an investment defines the often-quoted term *standard deviation.* It means what it says: the standard (read "average") deviation ("variation or difference") of a typical period's return from the average return. This will be reviewed in more detail later on, in the chapter dedicated to portfolio performance measurement.

How Hybrid Came to Be

We all know now that for investors, the first decade of the twenty-first century was strikingly different from the 1980s and 1990s. This came as a shock to many financial advisors and their clients, since most of them grew up in those roles during a period of consistently strong and resilient returns in stocks and bonds.

This gradually created a desire for investments that could either dampen volatility or provide positive returns in mixed or even down markets. Given the potential for continued choppiness in stocks and the specter of rising interest rates for bonds (which can lead to negative returns), the demand is understandable. But is it always necessary for advisors to delve into the world of hedge fund limited partnerships, managed futures funds, private equity, and the like? Do investors need to say goodbye to daily liquidity in order to say hello to low-correlation returns? My answer for some time has been a resounding no, and I am living proof of it.

During my time at Donaldson, Lufkin & Jenrette (1995–1998), I started to realize that the days of 30 percent annual returns in the stock market we experienced in the 1990s would not last forever. I have always been a student of financial market history and realized that while I could not predict when the stock market bubble would collapse, it ultimately would. Bubbles always burst.

In the late 1990s, I started a research effort with the goal of identifying mutual funds with strategies that used the stock and bond markets, but with protective measures in place—some call them "hedged" mutual funds; I called them "hybrids" because I see these investment approaches as having a component of growth as well as preservation captured within their style. While one could argue that this is true of any investment, the hybrid nature of these market areas is, in my opinion, more obvious and more specific. A fund manager that buys stocks of very small growth companies may believe that there is a preservation component to their portfolio, but unlike the styles we'll describe as hybrids, a big market decline has typically eroded a serious amount of value from those more volatile, equity-only styles. The evidence here is quite strong. Also, since I started using that name before hybrid automobiles and hybrid golf clubs hit the mainstream, I did not feel like I was a copycat.

I started running diversified portfolios containing these specialized funds. I became convinced that my team and I could deliver the kind of return that conservative hedge-funds-of-funds did, without some of the headaches that come with hedge funds. I have seen how well our hybrid strategy compares to the more conservative types of hedge funds, without a lot of the baggage that hedge funds carry in the eyes of investors.

As my team and I attended industry conferences over the years, there was a great deal of idea sharing. More and more, we were being told by our advisory peers that we had an investment philosophy that they would like to access. Over the next several years, we created a "deliverable" for them in the form of separate accounts, available through them for their clients, and later a mutual fund that combines the three styles. As a result, the emphasis of my work has changed over the years, from being an advisor and portfolio manager to a limited group of private clients to being an investment strategist for a wider audience, which still includes those clients. In summary, this intellectual property I developed for a decade was made available to the outside world, to both individual investors and through their financial advisors.

Many in my industry refer to the hybrid strategy as an "alternative" investment. It seems appropriate to ask, "an alternative to what?" If they mean an alternative to losing 55 percent on a stock index fund investment from the summer of 2008 through early March 2009, I think that definition is right on. However, I think you are better off viewing hybrid as not simply an alternative investment, but as one very critical part of an alternative approach to allocating assets in your portfolio.

The Objective of the Hybrid Allocation Strategy

The concrete, quantitative objective of the hybrid strategy is to produce a consistent stream of absolute returns with low market correlation over a minimum rolling three-year time period. I begin with the idea that the assets clients place under my care are not to simply accumulate, but to fund their future and/or current lifestyle. Many people do not want to see tremendous fluctuation in the possibility that they will achieve their desired lifestyle. It follows, then, that their portfolio should be designed to keep fluctuation in value low, while still maintaining the potential to grow at a competitive rate.

The hybrid strategy has three very specific objectives:

1. Pursue consistent positive returns with low volatility (beta).
2. Succeed with less dependency on the market itself (R-squared).
3. Shrink the range of possible outcomes (standard deviation).

My team and I accomplish this by researching a diverse group of investment styles, each of which is clearly distinguishable from traditional investment approaches. Then, we create a mix of those strategies that we feel provides the best chance of achieving the objectives mentioned earlier. We take a one- to three-year outlook on most of the holdings, but are opportunistic when a situation presents itself. In a more volatile market environment, price moves that used to take years may now occur in months, even weeks. In that case, if we have made money faster than we thought we would, we may take a short-term profit rather than be greedy. (You will notice that for a lot of what I say in this book, the phrase "rather than be greedy" applies.)

The hybrid model I originally created years ago has evolved significantly over time and continues to evolve today. The limited pool of funds from which we had to choose for potential investment many years ago has grown to well over 100 funds and counting. We have identified numerous additional investable hybrid styles and funds as time has gone by, and have added them to our research process.

Hybrid Mutual Fund Styles

Now that you have a brief history of how this "flagship" strategy called hybrid came to be, let's delve into the strategies that make up the hybrid universe as I define them. As a reminder, all of these are available in mutual fund form:

- *Long-short.* This is the original form of hedge fund investment. While the hedge fund industry has done much to obscure that proud history, the approach of buying what you like and shorting what you don't like is pretty logical. While there are similarities in style to hedge funds, long-short mutual funds do not use as much leverage (and that level is capped by law), keep costs reasonable, and are very often more tax efficient than hedge funds. They also offer daily liquidity.

- *Market-neutral.* Think long-short, but with an emphasis on keeping the longs and shorts close to even. This puts the emphasis on stock selection by the manager. Unlike the hedge fund version of this strategy, excessive leverage is not part of the plan. That's a good thing, I think.

- *Arbitrage.* When handled prudently, arbitrage is a wonderful thing. One gets the opportunity for consistent upside, but with built-in protection, since most deals a fund participates in involve both a long and short position (i.e., playing both sides of a merger event). I particularly like owning merger arbitrage in mutual fund form, as opposed to the highly leveraged hedge fund peers. This is a true hedge fund–like style, but in our preferred wrapper—an open-end mutual fund.

- *Convertible securities.* Convertibles, if chosen well, can provide the upside potential of the underlying stock, but with the "safety net" of a bond, since it is a bond until such time as it converts to the stock. The bond may carry an interest rate ("coupon"), or a company may issue a zero-coupon bond instead. Convertibles on their own are, in our judgment, the classic definition of a "hybrid" investment—is it a bond or a stock? Based on the potential outcomes of a convertible issue, we'd say the answer is "yes!" (i.e., it is both). In bull markets, equities should outperform convertibles, and the opposite is expected in bear cycles. Thus, this style embodies what I call the "flexible and adaptive" you should incorporate in your portfolio.

- *High-yield bonds.* Today, we call them high-yield bonds, though in the late 1980s they were commonly referred to as *junk bonds.* Back then, Wall Street infamy accrued to Michael Milken and Drexel Burnham, as the market they helped create, full of excessively leveraged deals and leveraged buyouts (LBOs), eventually collapsed. Bonds defaulted in large numbers, and the investment public swore off the sector until the mid-1990s. Coinciding with the dot-com bubble, tech and telecom companies issued medium- and low-quality corporate bonds. The market was revived, but took another step back during the three-year stock market decline from 2000 to 2002. Since 2003, the market for high-yield debt has reemerged as a viable investment market, at a more substantial size (about $800 billion) than in the past. High-yield bonds are where investors go to participate in the growth process for small to midsize companies, but through debt instead of equities. Many well-known companies now also issue high-yield bonds, and the default rates declined markedly as this investment segment matured. Today, we think it is fair to characterize high-yield bonds as a way to invest for growth with lower expected volatility than the stock market, but with a much higher cash flow return than equities typically provide.

- *Dedicated short equity.* Also called "bear funds," these can be very useful as part of an overall portfolio. When markets are expected to be range-bound or rising as the primary trend, we prefer to do any hedging with either single-short exchange-traded funds (ETFs) or index-short mutual funds, as the short positions in those cases are tactical.
- *Inverse bond.* As the name implies, these funds move inversely to the bond market. They can potentially profit from rising interest rates on U.S. Treasuries and even high-yield bonds. If you are an inflation hawk, that is a nice tool to add to your shed.
- *Global macro.* Myopic approaches that focus only on U.S. stocks, or on stocks and high-quality U.S. bonds only, are unnecessarily restricting themselves. This inflexibility can leave traditional "balanced funds" powerless in some markets. I am a firm believer that ultimate investment flexibility, in the hands of the right manager(s), is the key to long-term investment success. Some global macro funds offer that capability, and unlike traditional "balanced" funds, they are not limited to global stocks and high-quality bonds. The most attractive funds of this type look more like flexible hedge funds in a mutual fund package.
- *Currency.* Currency investing was the domain of Wall Street trading desks and hedge funds for many years, but several mutual funds are now available to U.S.-based investors to pursue growth of capital and income by owning bonds denominated in non-U.S. dollar currencies. The bonds' income is converted

into U.S. dollars, and if the currency appreciates against the U.S. dollar during the holding period, that income will convert into a higher return in U.S. currency than in the foreign currency, as the exchange rate to dollars favored the non-U.S. asset (the bond). The opposite is true when the U.S. dollar appreciates against the currency in which the bond is denominated. The idea of currency funds is to correctly forecast the direction of exchange rates, and profit from those forecasts through the use of government and corporate short-term debt in countries outside the United States.

- *Real estate investment trusts (REITs).* Real estate investing is not new to most Registered Investment Advisors (RIAs) and their clients. However, you have many avenues by which to pursue your real estate exposure. While both the public and private markets offer numerous and varied opportunities to participate, one look at the past couple of years in this sector, and you can understand why I believe that whatever the allure of the private markets, you can rest easier with daily liquidity. That applies to mutual funds that invest in U.S. REITs as well as those focused on international markets (see Figure 7.1).

Many of the best-performing funds in our portfolios are those whose styles allow for the most flexibility in the investment process. In other words, if you identify outstanding fund managers *and* give them the flexibility to go and make money in a risk-conscious way, they can add tremendous value (Wall Street sometimes calls this *alpha*) over traditional investment styles that are more restricted within the "style boxes." This is something we have seen over and

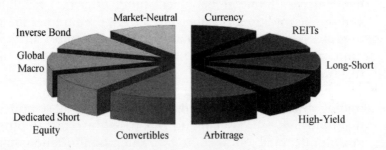

Figure 7.1   Sample Hybrid Strategy Allocation

over again in our observation of the hybrid asset class over the years. We understand that part of the process of creating an absolute return strategy involves owning something that will be down in value during the year. Why is this expected? Well, if a portfolio contains strategies that have low correlation to each other as well as the stock market, the chance of all of them going up or all of them going down in the same year is not likely. But by owning a diversified and noncorrelated group of assets, we get the smoother returns we are aiming for without having to trade in and out of funds aggressively as in a pure timing strategy.

Constructing Hybrid Portfolios

Now that you have been introduced to the possible "players" in a hybrid portfolio, let's discuss how to put the best players on the field at a particular time, and how to make them work together as a team so you can win.

Advisors and their clients have devised an infinite number of asset allocation models in search of the right of mix of these investments. During the 1990s, strong returns were common, as the stock and bond markets performed well. It was tough to fail.

It is a portfolio of no-load mutual funds and balancing strategies carefully chosen and managed. These funds are judged by us to have hedge fund–like qualities, seeking returns that approach those of stocks with far less expected volatility.

In summary, hybrid investing is similar to the multimanager approach used by market-neutral and opportunistic hedge-funds-of-funds. However, by using mutual funds that employ hedge fund–like strategies, I can deliver to the investor a similar experience as hedge-funds-of-funds in terms of absolute return, but absent many of the headaches of funds-of-funds. The advantages of this strategy include lower total cost, much greater liquidity, greater transparency, greater tax-efficiency, and more overall flexibility in the process.

The Hybrid Investment Process

The hybrid investment process is fourfold: First, I screen the universe of all mutual funds to arrive at a list of those which pursue strategies that best represent our definition of the hybrid approach.

Second, I determine for each subsector of the hybrid universe (e.g., REITs, long-short, arbitrage, etc.) whether we should be equal weight, overweight, or underweight the allocation of our Emerald Hybrid Index.

Third, I select for the portfolio a combination of funds that I feel offer the best prospects for competitive positive returns with low volatility and correlation compared to the broad stock market, in a tax-efficient manner. Again, this is a strategy for those investors who view investing as a tool to help achieve their desired lifestyle instead of relying on whatever the market provides to them as an outcome.

Finally, I continually monitor these holdings with my team. Detailed analysis may reveal reasons to consider or execute changes to the model. Recall that in the last chapter I listed several typical reasons for exiting an existing position.

The various fundamental and technical indicators used in analyzing funds also result in differing levels of confidence to us. For instance, if gross domestic product (GDP) is very strong for a quarter, that quarter is not looked at as a trend. As long-term investors, we put more emphasis on trends that have been established and confirmed, not events that could ultimately be determined to be "outliers" or temporary noise in the long run.

As our process is more than simply producing a quantitative conclusion and acting on it, our indicators and weightings are always subject to change based on new information. Weightings, as with our sell process in general, may change based on factors related to overall market fluctuation, changes of personnel and management at a fund, when we determine that our investment thesis is wrong, or that an idea that we saw high potential for has run its course, or under other circumstances, according to the client's best interests.

Because I focus on absolute return over any three-year period, my goal is to make money for my investors regardless of market conditions. Therefore, we are largely environment neutral. However, from an absolute return standpoint, the portfolios I construct tend to make their highest returns on the "coattails" of a surging stock market. From a relative return standpoint, the more the stock market declines, the more hybrid portfolios are expected to outperform the broad stock market benchmarks.

It is reasonable to expect our hybrid portfolios to achieve a standard deviation that is noticeably less than that of the S&P

500. Our turnover historically has been between 25 percent and 75 percent per year. That is, we replace between one-fourth and three-fourths of the portfolio each year. The exception to this was in 2008, when market gyrations forced us to be much more nimble than ever before, just to post returns in the neighborhood of breakeven.

We do not use the "portfolio optimization" models that are so popular in our industry, as to us, optimization is a stab at perfection that will never be realized. But we do run our models through a back-test system as described earlier. When we do this, we are looking particularly for data such as best/worst performance in a period, alpha, beta, and R-squared, that is, our volatility control measures and the portfolio's potential to deliver returns not highly correlated to the stock market.

In developing and refining the hybrid models, I use a combination of fundamental analysis (both top-down and bottom-up), quantitative analysis, and technical analysis.

- *Top-down.* Determination of the allocation to each hybrid subsector.
- *Bottom-up.* Selection of funds that are attractive hybrid investments.
- *Quantitative.* Factors such as dividend rate, turnover, expense ratio, and embedded unrealized capital gains in a fund are all considered in the evaluation of a fund for the models.
- *Technical.* Once the other screening methods have been completed, charting analysis has been a very useful tool for us to determine the best entry and exit points for a fund, as well as to analyze general market conditions. This was discussed in the last chapter.

Where Hybrid Investing Fits into Your Portfolio

As time has passed, I have learned much about how to best position the hybrid strategy within a client's overall portfolio. I can say with confidence that hybrid, along with the other strategies I manage, represents to investors and investment advisors an alternative to:

- Bond funds and bond managed accounts
- Target-date funds

- Balanced portfolios
- Conservative hedge funds and hedge-funds-of-funds

As part of an independent firm, I am able to access a wide range of resources for research and analysis purposes. Also, as I stated at the beginning of this book, I read many of my industry's trade publications. In addition, my frequent appearance in the print media has attracted much attention from the hedge fund and mutual fund industries. Firms of all shapes and sizes send information to us about their products. This helps us stay quite current on what is being offered in the less liquid/higher-cost/less transparent segment of our peer group, and helps us continually refine the hybrid strategies.

Benchmarking the Performance of the Hybrid Allocation Strategy

For performance benchmarking purposes, I primarily use the Dow Jones Conservative Allocation Index. While it is not very widely known, it seems to us to capture the spirit of the conservative style in which I manage hybrid portfolios. Importantly, the index includes only traditional stock and bond components, with a heavy tilt toward the latter. Still, it allows me to gauge how much value we are adding for the investor versus what they might have invested in if they had never met us—namely, a portfolio that maintained a high bond weighting, with some equity market exposure. As with all strategies I manage, the broad stock market index, S&P 500, is a benchmark we follow. Here, however, the idea is to compare how we do in up and down markets (see Chapter 10 on performance measurement and capture ratios).

In a strong, sustainable bull market for stocks, hybrid should not be expected to keep pace. Its value versus an equity-oriented investment is best evidenced by our ability to limit the damage in down markets and get a decent piece of the up markets, such that over longer periods of time (such as the latter part of last decade), hybrid is competitive with an equity-oriented portfolio, but with far lower volatility along the way.

We will also compare hybrid performance to that of a standard, broad market fixed-income index. I have found that over time, hybrid can be an effective substitute for some or all of an actively managed high-quality bond investment. I suspect that if I do my job going forward, this will become even more obvious in an environment of rising interest rates/falling bond prices.

Risk Management in the Hybrid Strategy

Hybrid is a conservatively managed portfolio with an absolute return focus. At the top level, risk is managed by the design and construction of hybrid's fund-of-funds approach. I diversify across multiple alternative strategies/styles whose economic return drivers may differ and who tend to exhibit low correlation with one another. I use multiple managers (generally 8 to 15) to avoid single-manager risk. In addition, each of these managers is applying some hedging to his or her own portfolios. I have the flexibility to use the short side of the market at the portfolio level (through dedicated short funds) to hedge the portfolio even further and potentially protect against downside risk. I will adjust our cash position as we see fit and may use cash as a defensive weapon. I employ an ongoing due diligence process in which we actively monitor our managers. This includes a strict sell discipline for all the managers we employ, as explained earlier.

In addition to the numerous aspects of the risk control system noted above, I have established other guidelines, along with my colleagues, to reduce volatility. For example, we do not typically take a position of more than 20 percent in one fund (at cost) or 25 percent at market value. I will typically not invest more than 30 percent of the fund (at cost) in any one substyle of hybrid (REITs, arbitrage, etc.). This is for protective, not speculative, purposes. I want to reserve the right to shield the client from a down stock market of historic proportions. There were periods during 2008 and early 2009 where the dedicated short position in all of our portfolio strategies were at their all-time highs. In particular, the hybrid strategy actually spent part of this period being "net short" the stock market—that is, it was positioned such that a falling stock market would be expected to produce gains in the hybrid strategy. This is a state of the portfolio that we consider very carefully and don't stay with for too long. Why? Because in my mind, the only thing worse than losing money in a down market is losing money in an up market!

As you can tell from the preceding description, the key to this risk-control methodology is also the key to the overall approach:

investment flexibility. Unlike the vast majority of the investment management peers, I do not put hard constraints on myself because the motivation for using a hybrid approach is to minimize the negative aspects of traditional investing. However, despite the flexibility, there is a discipline that we follow to keep portfolio fluctuations as low as possible without significantly impacting growth potential.

When creating or changing a hybrid portfolio, it is necessary to consider the possibility of a worst-case scenario. We run back-tests of our models to see what their worst case has been, then make a discretionary judgment as to what could make it worse.

For instance, the vast majority of strategists in the business today did not manage money during the last sustained period of rising interest rates (which ended 25 years ago). I also analyze past trades to see why they worked or didn't work in this model. I look at what the technical analysis was telling us as well as the fundamental analysis. What I look for is to make sure our thought process is consistent (though this does not mean we were always correct in our analysis). I have been preparing for the possibility that the rules of investing, as this generation knows them, will change if the secular decline in rates has finally reversed itself. Past history may not reflect what will happen in the future, but it certainly can be one factor in our modeling process, so we use it. I also analyze past trades to see why they worked or didn't work in this model. I look at what the technical analysis, as well as the fundamental analysis, was telling us. What I look for is to make sure our thought process is consistent (though this does not mean I was always correct in my analysis).

Managing portfolios in this "alternative" fashion is something I have been doing since before it was fashionable. In fact, I still don't see that the advisory business has been nearly as active in the hybrid asset class as it should be. I believe my team and I are a step or two ahead of our industry because we have become very familiar with who the hybrid managers are, which ones have a process that promotes success, and where to look next for opportunity. In addition the balancing act we refer to within the portfolio (allocating to a number of strategies that are influenced very differently by the same market events) is something that can come only with experience, in our opinion. As the creators of a very comprehensive hybrid portfolio strategy, we feel that we are in as good a position as any advisor in the industry to direct portfolios of this nature.

Hybrid Investing: A Flagship Strategy for Twenty-First-Century Asset Allocation

So, hybrid portfolios are in the business of reducing pain while still allowing for great progress. The natural balancing of many different and uncorrelated investment styles within the same portfolio provides a strong solution for those investors who are concerned about their financial future hanging on where the stock market and interest rates go next. I feel we provide an all-weather portfolio that can be appropriate for many investor needs. Because of our relatively long experience, we believe we will be on the cutting edge as this investment strategy continues to evolve and gain ground.

I believe hybrid provides advisors and their investors with a solid foundation for many portfolios, and one that can make a great addition to strategies that are managed with more aggressive risk-reward characteristics. It is designed for the investor who embraces the importance and philosophy of playing adequate offense, but playing better defense. This means sacrificing some of the equity market's upside in order to be on guard and better positioned for market declines. While all of the strategies I have created over the years aim for this outcome, hybrid is the one most vigilant against market risk.

Hybrid investment evaluation is a cumulative process taking into account stock market valuation ratios (price-to-earnings, price-to-book, yield, etc.), bond interest rates (from short-term rates through 30-year maturities), broad and narrow economic indicators (broad such as the Consumer Price Index/Producer Price Index, productivity, trade and budget deficits, etc.; narrow such as expected adjustments in adjustable-rate mortgages over the next year, for example).

Because the hybrid strategy spans such a wide variety of markets, my colleagues and I closely track indicators that have particular relevance to one or more substyles within the hybrid world. For example, merger-and-acquisition activity impacts arbitrage strategies. Corporate default rates impact high-yield bonds, short interest impacts the upside and downside potential of the stock market, and a long list of factors influence commodity prices.

Within the hybrid strategy, the most important risk-control method is the nature of the strategy itself. A central tenet to hybrid investing is that the combination of funds owned will have several natural offsets to each other. There is some stock shorting in the portfolio that neutralizes risk versus an all-stock portfolio. The use of styles such as arbitrage and market-neutral greatly reduces the impact of stock market movements. The ability to short the bond market or currencies via mutual funds allows us to offset some of the client's exposure to interest-rate-sensitive segments of the portfolio.

To summarize, hybrid investing is a risk-control vehicle to begin with. My job is to make as high a return as is prudently possible, given the natural constraints of the style.

Why Not Just Pick One Alternative Mutual Fund and Call It a Day?

I have been asked this question many times. My answer is simple and backed up by considerable evidence. If you choose any single fund, which represents a single style, you still have the risk of that one style. If you select only one fund (say a market-neutral or arbitrage mutual fund), you may leave a lot of money on the table, as the long-term returns may be limited in those styles, which are at the conservative end of hybrid (which means *very* conservative).

If you instead select a single fund that contains multiple styles, but all run through the same firm and same investment brains, you have a lesser but still concerning version of the situation I just described.

This is why I advocate the multistyle, multimanager approach outlined as the hybrid strategy in this chapter. After all, for many investors (the more conservative ones), hybrid investing should play a *core* role in their portfolio, not a peripheral one. For others, hybrid is simply part of the puzzle. But selecting a single fund or single style within the hybrid space is unnecessarily risky, for the same reason as buying only small-cap stocks across your whole portfolio. The age-old adage of diversification is still critical, as long as it is smart diversification. That has been my conclusion over many years of trial and error "their way" before creating and refining the hybrid strategy into what it is today.

I have been researching and allocating among alternative investment styles using mutual funds (and more recently, ETFs) since way before it was fashionable or even common. To me, these are effectively "alternatives to alternative investing." As emphasized throughout this book, I think you may find that alternative investing through mutual funds can carry a good portion of the load for you.

In my opinion, stocks, bonds, and cash do not provide adequate diversification in today's market environment. A more flexible approach that includes hybrid styles is required. Note that, very often, hybrid investing is not a substitute for stock and bond investments. It is a complement to them. In other cases, investors have told me that they are most comfortable in a portfolio that is primarily hybrid oriented.

I view hybrids as the "core" asset class in our clients' portfolios. Stocks and bonds are secondary, or "satellite," parts of the overall plan. This is the opposite of how most advisors view the world. This tends to make my strategy very complementary with theirs, though it can also function as a substitute for "traditional" portfolio construction.

Hybrid strategies have proven the ability to persevere through difficult environments for stocks, bonds, or both. Put another way, "there's always a bull market somewhere." That somewhere could be in convertible securities, arbitrage strategies, or even in shorting a major market (for instance, buying funds that short stocks will allow us to benefit from a falling stock market—i.e., a bull market for shorting). This shows clearly that the investor's best friend now and always is *flexibility* in the investment process.

CHAPTER 8

Concentrated Equity Investing

As you now know, I started touting the benefits of hybrid mutual funds long before investors, industry media, and the fund industry itself began to pay attention to them. The same is true with the second of the three portfolio allocation strategies I manage, concentrated equity. Finally, after years of playing second fiddle to overdiversified ("de-worse-ified") equity funds, the benefits of owning fewer stocks in a manager's portfolio are being recognized. I suppose a year like 2008 acts like a heavy rainstorm. Ideas and concepts finally make their way to the surface, like worms on the sidewalk after that storm.

My Favorite Article on Concentrated Mutual Fund Investing

The *Wall Street Journal*'s Larry Light wrote an article on October 9, 2009, entitled "OK, Now Concentrate." The subtitle of the article said, "Some managers run focused funds with 40 or fewer stocks. That approach can make performance more volatile—but, surprisingly, not always." I have always been a big fan of the *Wall Street Journal,* and now I am a fan of Larry Light and his editors, too. In a small number of words, he summarized this entire chapter, and the entire concept of concentrated equity investing. It is a useful strategy, but requires a more comprehensive research effort than simply picking funds off a performance list. I will explain that as this chapter continues.

For Mr. Light's article, the *Wall Street Journal* requested a research study from fund analysis and rating firm Morningstar Inc.

Morningstar looked at the performance and volatility of stock funds with 40 or fewer holdings as of the most recent portfolio (at that time) in Morningstar's database. Here is some of what they discovered and said, as noted in the article:

> As a group, these funds haven't consistently outperformed or underperformed funds with more diverse holdings.
>
> Based on recent performance and an earlier Morningstar study, concentrated funds aren't more volatile than more diversified funds, on average, and some are surprisingly steady despite their small number of holdings.
>
> The concentrated-fund concept flies in the face of a key tenet of investing—diversification, which is aimed at spreading risk and maximizing opportunity to latch onto winners. Most stock funds adopt the safety-in-numbers approach, with an average of about 180 stocks, according to Morningstar.
>
> Managers of scantly populated portfolios say their key advantage is they can more easily zero in on a limited number of names, drilling deeply into each, thus minimizing the chances of unpleasant surprises and maximizing the odds of finding gems.
>
> A concentrated portfolio clearly has the potential to make returns more volatile. With fewer stocks, a fund's performance may be tied to fewer parts of the economy.
>
> Still, a Morningstar study of performance from 1992 through 2006 found that volatility was fairly close between the least and the most concentrated funds, as measured by standard deviation, a gauge of how much returns differ from the average over time. Although that massive study hasn't been updated, the average returns of focus funds and more diversified funds over the past three years are close enough to suggest not much has changed.

This article and the excerpts noted above are the perfect segue to a description of the concentrated equity asset allocation strategy. First, it's true that many mutual funds whose portfolios are concentrated have done a mediocre or poor job over the years. But no one here is talking about buying an index of concentrated funds. In fact, it is just the opposite. This type of fund selection process is one that seeks to truly understand what the management team is trying to do, within the boundaries that a portfolio with a limited number of stocks allows.

In addition, the "steady" managers in this space are steady for a reason: they are simply better than the average, so they make fewer mistakes. If they start making more mistakes, they perform worse. It's pretty straightforward. Concentrated equity management is primarily a skill game, not over a month or a year, but over a multi-year period.

When Does Diversification Lose Its Benefits?

In general, I am not a big fan of the so-called Modern Portfolio Theory (MPT), in which risk and reward are mathematically balanced to produce a so-called optimal portfolio. The theory concludes that allocating assets effectively is about number crunching to find the "efficient" combination of reward (return) and risk (measured by standard deviation, or how an investment's returns of different periods compare to that investment's long-term average return). I think that the number-crunching, backward-looking analysis in MPT is a decent starting point, but leaves way too much on the table. I prefer to look at risk as a combination of measures, as you will discover later in the book in the chapter on measuring performance.

The philosophy behind the approach of using concentrated equity portfolios is academic, and it has been supported by numerous examples over the years. Studies have been done that analyze the optimal level of diversification within an all-stock portfolio, the goal being to avoid "overdiversification" (which I referred to earlier in the book as "de-worse-ification"). While many investors believe that risk is proportionately reduced with each additional stock in a portfolio, there is evidence that you can only reduce your risk to a certain point after which there is no further benefit from diversification.

In my experience, I have seen that, indeed, many of the most successful equity managers—those who have outperformed and who have generated consistent alpha over time—are those who have focused on a smaller number of stocks (see Figure 8.1).

Does this mean that you should pick one concentrated equity manager and go with them? No. Several years ago, I started to survey the universe of equity mutual funds, to see how prevalent this

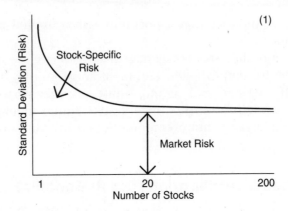

Figure 8.1 The Diminishing Benefits of Diversification within a Manager's Portfolio as More Stocks Are Added

Source: Investopedia

concentrated approach was. I did find enough funds to start a re-search "universe" of them, and I set out to determine their attract-iveness. The result of that effort was a set of conclusions similar to that stated in the *Wall Street Journal* article mentioned earlier. Just as there are winners and losers in the universe of international stock funds, small-cap funds, value funds, real estate investment trust (REIT) funds, and so on, there are winners and losers in the con-centrated equity fund segment of the marketplace.

When I say winners and losers, I am not referring to past per-formance. As you will learn in Chapter 10, anyone can review a set of fund returns and draw conclusions. But unless you are in a 1990s-style bull market bonanza, those conclusions will be incomplete, and your assumptions and extrapolations of that return data may cost you a lot of money. Instead, equity funds that concentrate their holdings should be viewed as a subasset class within the universe of equity funds, and the analysis of them should be directed at the fund manager's experience in running concentrated portfolios, the validity of the style in which they manage, the likelihood of success in different market environments, and so on.

Here is a good example of what I mean. As 2008 was nearing its end, my team and I became more confident that the global equity markets, which had fallen over 40 percent within the past 12 months, were in a valuation zone that lent itself to a bit of "toe-dipping." It was time for us to gradually increase our equity exposure versus holding high short positions and a lot of cash. Over the next few months, we began to increase our equity exposure within our concentrated equity portfolio, but it was how we did it that was the notable part. We bought a couple of funds that we had not owned in the past, though we had researched them for some time. We knew their strengths and weaknesses, their tendencies, and their style belief. We also had a good grasp of how they were allocated, the stocks they owned, and how likely they were to turn the portfolio over significantly. In both cases, they were traditionally low-turnover funds, and in our discussions with the managers themselves, we found no reason to believe that would change.

With the bulk of our fund-specific work having been done well before we considered buying these funds, we went back to the macro-rationale for buying them at that point, in late 2008. Our "weight of the evidence" analysis determined that the reward of taking modest positions in these two concentrated funds, using our hoard of cash that had built up during 2008's market nightmare, was worth the risks we had identified. In our minds, the risk was largely limited to the general nature of equity investing and the tenuous overall stock market environment at the time. We felt we had the right managers all along, and now we also felt that it was time to step in and use them.

This story had a very happy ending, at least over the next 12 months. Both funds did extremely well, even better than we had expected, and even considering the market's dramatic gains during the year. But that is not the point. The reason I pulled the trigger on the purchases in late 2008 was our feeling that if the market was gradually entering a kinder environment, it was the right time to own funds that, if we were right about the market's new trend, would be very good long-term investments. As it was, we bought one of the funds at more than 65 percent below its high price of the previous year. Great management we are confident in with a better market condition approaching was a powerful combination that had not existed in the prior 18 months that we had been following these funds. Now, things were different, so made our move.

The point of this example is that choosing concentrated equity funds, like choosing other types of funds, is a research-intensive process. I do think that this is a fading art within the investment business. Morningstar and other fund analysis firms are heavy on the data, but do not follow the funds like Wall Street analysts follow stocks of public companies. I think the gap between those two processes should be narrowed. But we live in a sound-bite world, so the act of truly digging into the story so you know you are buying more than a pile of data is foreign to many industry professionals.

I understand why in the case of financial advisors. Their role as a communicator, client service provider and advocate, and advisor, on top of their more demanding compliance and business-building responsibilities, does not allow for the level of ongoing fund analysis that they would probably prefer to do. I think that is a big reason why my firm and I have been an attractive research and portfolio management outsource tool for financial advisors around the United States.

For the individual, the time may be there. The question is: do they have the experience and skills to make good long-term decisions, or are they only as good as or a little bit better than what the market allows them to be? They are handicapped somewhat by their limited access to the management team. Advisors have a distinct advantage here. They are viewed as "institutional" investors by the fund companies, as when they buy, they often buy in "bulk" size, across their client base. Just as in the pension fund world, the bigger the client, the bigger the attention that can be paid when access to key personnel is desired by the client. This is no different from most other parts of the business world, of course.

At my firm's weekly research meetings, we typically devote a portion of the agenda to a live interview with a manager from one of the funds we own or are researching. When it comes to mutual fund research, there is nothing like hearing it from the horse's mouth! That is also why, to the extent I am able, I make myself available to financial advisors who are considering our separate-account strategies or mutual fund. I sympathize with their efforts to do a thorough due-diligence job for their clients.

What Is the Concentrated Equity Allocation Strategy?

Now that you know the rationale behind concentrated equity mutual fund investing, and we know that there are a sufficient number of quality funds to choose from in my self-created concentrated equity mutual fund slice of the fund world, we can now move on to the specifics of how my team and I operate in this area.

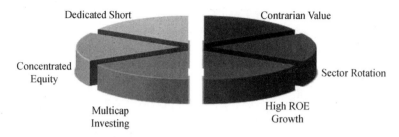

Figure 8.2   Sample Concentrated Equity Strategy Allocation

This strategy aims to take moderate risk, tag along with up markets, play good defense in down markets, and by that combination succeed over a period of three to five years. As you probably realize by now, this approach is similar across everything I have created and managed. The strategies mainly differ as to what investment styles are used, the time horizon involved, and especially the level of risk and volatility that is expected to occur, in both the short term and long term (see Figure 8.2).

How Many Stock Holdings Makes a Fund "Concentrated?"

This is subject to interpretation by the user, but to me, a fund that owns 30 stocks or less fits the definition. There are certainly exceptions, particularly when considering the more esoteric areas such as microcap stocks (smaller than small cap, where the risk of a single position is expected to be even greater than for a small cap fund, since microcap companies are less liquid and often underfollowed by analysts).

The key is not to find one manager you think is great and give them all of your equity allocation. Instead, I strongly recommend that you diversify across multiple concentrated equity managers, each of whom has a particular edge in their specific area of focus. This includes various segments of the equity arena, such as contrarian value, high return-on-equity (ROE) growth, multicap investing, and sector rotation.

Minimizing overlap is clearly a goal in constructing these portfolios. There have been times where our portfolio owned seven different funds, each with at least 20 positions, and there was not a single common position among any two of the funds. We test this through analytical software, and while it's not a perfect exercise, since mutual funds' full holdings are typically made public quarterly, it is an analysis we are confident in.

We may also utilize a dedicated short equity manager or "inverse exchange-traded fund (ETF)" as a means of potentially reducing volatility and hedging the portfolio. This feature of the portfolio cannot be underestimated! It is probably the single biggest differentiator between the way I view equity investing and how an individual manager, concentrated or not, views it. To me, the "ace in the hole" for us is that instead of simply raising cash when attractive candidates are scarce, or making up excuses for poor bear market performance, such as "we own great stocks and/or funds, so in time we'll succeed," we can do something about it. We can hedge risk. In doing so, I have much greater control of the portfolio's "net long exposure," that is, how sensitive the portfolio will be to movements up or down in the overall stock market. As with all of the strategies I manage, this net long exposure can be managed as frequently as I want, simply by adjusting that hedge position.

At the same time, we can continue to hold our favorite long-term fund positions, which may allow us to produce far more long-term capital gains than short-term gains. Having that ability to short "in our back pocket" at all times is a weapon we can use to reduce the portfolio's overall volatility, which is closely related to the concept of playing great defense. As I have said many times in this book, it is essential to avoid the big loss. Well, how do you do that in a portfolio like concentrated equity, which aims for long-term growth, benchmarks itself to the broad stock market (S&P 500 Index), and shies away from playing outright "market-timing" games? How do you do it? You give yourself permission to hedge as needed. It sounds like a straightforward concept—because it is. Yet, the vast majority of portfolio managers and asset allocators don't employ it. As I said earlier, that 1990s mentality is very tough to break—for them.

More about the Concentrated Equity Investment Process

Today, we maintain our own database of funds that meet the definition of a "concentrated equity" discipline. The portfolio construction process applies bottom-up fundamental analysis to continually identify the most compelling managers, and the ones selected are each focused on different areas of the equity markets. The goal is to find a blend of strong, alpha-generating managers who are pursuing different means to accomplish their goals, thereby minimizing any potential overlap among them. Quantitative analysis is applied to help determine fund weightings, and technical analysis is used to assist in determining buy and sell points.

The pattern I have found in most, though not all, of the managers I am attracted to is that the managers view their holdings as businesses they can own for a long period of time. They tend to favor conducting thorough company research rather than analysis of short-term market factors. While each manager's relatively small number of holdings may produce shorter-term volatility than a broad-based strategy, I attempt to lower portfolio volatility by diversifying among a group of five to eight managers.

For the concentrated equity portfolio, potential funds are evaluated based on their three- to five-year return potential. As you probably realize by now, the short position is far more dynamic. In some years I may invoke it several times a year, and in other years, I may not use it at all. That is the beauty of the flexible/adaptive theme that underlies this entire book. Instead of being compelled to hedge when hedging is not worth the risk (in this case, the risk of not grabbing as much of the market's up move as you could), I can continue to hold that ability to short in my back pocket, but not use it simply to use it. Whether I short to hedge, or don't short to increase the potential upside participation, I can add value, on top of what the underlying concentrated fund managers in the portfolio do. The same goes for the use of cash, raising or lowering it as needed, as often or as seldom as I feel is required to stay on track toward the strategy's long-term objectives.

Sell Discipline

All managers are actively monitored, as are funds that may represent potential new or replacement positions. Reasons for terminating a manager may include the following:

- A fund has become too large.
- A fund company has become too "institutionalized."
- There are turnover and/or material personnel changes on the investment team.
- A fund has exhibited style drift.

- There is lagging performance for unexplainable reasons.
- Our investment thesis was wrong.

I think concentrated equity provides investors and financial advisors with a solid equity foundation for many portfolios, and one that may make a valuable addition to strategies that are managed with more conservative and more aggressive risk-reward characteristics. Concentrated equity can be used as a core equity holding that may complement more conservative and more aggressive strategies. It diversifies across multiple equity managers, yet unlike traditional long-only strategies, it has the flexibility to hedge the portfolio and/or use cash liberally. Thus, I believe concentrated equity can be used as an attractive alternative to core equity funds, moderate allocation strategies, 130/30 funds, long/short equity funds, and target-date funds.

Benchmarking the Performance of the Concentrated Equity Allocation Strategy

Concentrated equity portfolios are, at their core, similar to traditional equity portfolios. They just have greater flexibility to hedge, and they espouse a philosophy that concentration in a manager's stock portfolio produces better long-term results than a highly diversified portfolio. Thus, the traditional stock market benchmarks are used by us to evaluate the performance of this strategy. The S&P 500 is the most widely used stock market benchmark in the United States, and so we use it for these portfolios. While concentrated equity portfolios may contain mutual funds that have a portion of their assets in non-U.S. stocks, this is not a key part of the strategy's mandate. Thus, a U.S. equity benchmark is the best choice here.

This is not so for the last of the three strategies I created and manage, global cycle. Let's move on to Chapter 9 and you will see why.

CHAPTER 9

Global Cycle Investing

MARKET CYCLES: A KEY TO UNDERSTANDING YOUR ODDS AS A LONG-TERM INVESTOR

I have devoted many years and hours to the study of stock market cycles. Understanding first that market and economic cycles exist, and also how they influence what investment approaches are successful at different points in time, is vital to nearly any investor. The benefit is that by simply knowing what is possible, you can gauge what level of portfolio risk you are willing to take on at different points in the cycle.

The study of market cycles could fill a library by itself. There is vital information for today's investor and financial advisor in the conclusions that have been made by those who devote time to studying such things. The scope of the issues of market cycles is far beyond the limits of this book. However, the conclusions are not. I suspect it is very likely that you are reading this book more because "you want to know what time it is" and not because "you want to know how the watch is made"—that is, you want to know what to do, not find out exactly how it's done and do it all over again by yourself. So, I will try to communicate a bit of the history of market cycle studies and focus more on the conclusions. After all, in my day-to-day work involving market cycles, I seek to identify secular trends and then determine how best to pursue them through investing. That is, in a nutshell, what the global cycle strategy is about.

The business cycle or economic cycle is the periodic ups and downs in activity within a long-term period, such that a trend results. The cycle involves shifts over time between two alternating types of time periods:

1. Periods of relatively rapid growth of market prices (if we are referring to stocks, bonds, commodities, etc.) or output (recovery and prosperity in the economy)
2. Periods of relative stagnation or decline (contraction or recession)

Some would argue that one of roles of government is to try to smooth out the business and economic cycles, reducing its fluctuations. While I think that one should lead a "balanced life" to avoid emotional ups and downs (and boy, is that critical in my business!), I will not dare to enter the long-running debate on whether political leaders should have a hand in the solution. I will leave that to CNN, FOX, and MSNBC to battle out on a nightly basis.

It does appear that the lengths of these cycles (from peak to peak, or from trough to trough) do vary, so that cycles are not uniform or mechanical in their regularity. Since no two cycles are alike in their details, some economists dispute the existence of cycles and use the word *fluctuations* (or the like) instead. As far as you and I are concerned, there appears to be plenty of evidence that can be summarized as follows: in the markets and the economy, history does not repeat, but it sure does rhyme! And we are talking about investing via a strategy (global cycle) whose underlying tenets take a long time to develop; there is some "wiggle room" to interpret whether we are right or wrong along the way.

To me, the greatest value of the global cycle strategy is the ability to take a step back, look at investing as a "big picture" exercise, and make adjustments along the way. As you might have guessed, this brings us right back to the concepts of investing discussed throughout this book, in particular, the ability to hedge one's position during shorter, "countertrend" declines in stock prices, while holding onto your core long-term positions, as well as the ability to adjust positions up and down, while staying committed to them for the long-run. With hedging tools available within the broader context of long-term strategy, you have a better shot at getting what you want.

Types of Business Cycles

So business cycles exist and we can use that knowledge to make investment decisions. At this point, you are probably thinking, "Okay, that's all I need to know about that." But there is one more part to the story. As it turns out, there are several different types of cycles, and when you realize what they are, the three main investment time frames investment strategists and portfolio managers talk about make total sense.

We refer to "tactical" investing as something that is done in pursuit of shorter-term profits. To me, a tactical decision is one made with the expectation of a profit within 90 days of purchase. I am sure that is not the only definition, given the thousands of hedge fund and tactical mutual fund managers around.

"Cyclical" investing, as I define it, covers periods longer than tactical, and up to a few years in length. "Secular" investing covers several years, a decade, or even spans more than one decade. Apparently, those who have studied investment and business cycles over the past couple of centuries have theorized some of the underlying causes of those different investment lengths. Each is named after the person that identified it. For instance:

- *Kitchin inventory cycle (3–5 years): Named after Joseph Kitchin.* [*] A Kitchin cycle is a short business cycle of about 40 months, discovered in the 1920s by Joseph Kitchin.

  Think about what happens in the economy on a regular basis. There are times when finding a job is not too difficult, because economic activity is in expansion mode. Plenty of consumer items are being produced, and the demand for them gets higher and higher (flat-screen TVs are a good post-2008 example). At some point, the demand for those items cannot possibly keep up the supply of them, as the economy is imperfect and plenty of companies will be late to the party.

  What happens next? Demand for flat-screens starts to fall, and panicked retailers and suppliers cut their prices, and inventories of those flat-screen TVs start to pile up in

---

[*] *Source:* Andrey V. Korotayev and Sergey V. Tsirel, "A Spectral Analysis of World GDP Dynamics: Kondratieff Waves, Kuznets Swings, Juglar and Kitchin Cycles in Global Economic Development, and the 2008–2009 Economic Crisis." *Structure and Dynamics,* 4(1), 2010.

warehouses. Price cutting only goes so far, and eventually the companies that produce the TVs decide it's time to cut the amount they will produce, while retailers start to order fewer of them. However, this process takes some time. It takes some time for the information that the supply is way ahead of the demand to get to the business community. Also, the decision to cut production does not happen immediately, as decision makers take time to make sure they are making the right move and the proper degree.

Similarly, they don't "ring a bell" when it's the right time to ramp up production again and hire more workers, as inventories have gradually diminished. Thus, decision makers must analyze that decision, too. I think you get the idea: these types of cycles are ingrained in both human nature and the reality of the business world. Thus, Kitchin cycles, which conclude that it takes roughly three to three and a half years to see such a cycle through, explain a lot of what we see in the shorter-term business cycle. It follows that the investment markets, which watch closely every day for the next clue on this type of activity, through reports from companies and government statistics, are prone to this type of cyclical behavior, too.

- *Juglar fixed investment cycle (7–11 years): Named after Clement Juglar.*[*] When economists talk about the "business cycle," this is what they are usually referring to. Recovery and prosperity are associated with increases in productivity, consumer confidence, aggregate demand, and prices. In the cycles before World War II or that of the late 1990s in the United States, the growth periods usually ended with the failure of speculative investments built on a bubble of confidence that bursts or deflates. Does that remind you of anything you saw starting in 2000 and again in late 2007? You betcha.

  These cycles are accentuated by waves of optimism and pessimism, in which upturns lead to expectations of even better times to come, and downturns to panics in anticipation of worse to follow. Simple models of the business cycle suggest that these fluctuations should occur at regular intervals, but historically they have varied greatly in length and scale. This makes it extremely difficult to stabilize them by monetary or

---

[*]*Source:* encyclopedia.stateuniversity.com/pages/3434/business-cycle.html.

fiscal policy, especially since the public authorities themselves are subject to waves of optimism and pessimism about the economy.

In other words, politicians have a habit of getting too emotional about these things—as if you didn't know. Add to that the fact that they are running for reelection every two to six years, and you have on your hands a moving target (Washington's power brokers) trying to harness another moving target (the business cycle). Good luck with that! The good news is that we, as investors, can take advantage of that chaos, instead of simply falling in line with the many market participants who become victims of each cyclical decline.

- *Kuznets infrastructural (building and real estate valuation) investment cycle (15–25 years): Named after Nobel laureate Simon Kuznets.* John Serrapere, the brilliant writer of Arrow Insights (www. arrowinsights.com) wrote about the work of Nobel laureate Simon Kuznets in a November 2009 commentary: Kuznets held a thesis that identified infrastructure expenditures as being the primary driver of a 15- to 25-year real/financial asset cycle. In the Kuznets cycle, transportation, public service, and utility structures are in periodic need of major revisions, replacement, and/or new construction. These expenditures accelerate demand for basic materials and industrial supplies, which leads to higher commodity prices, increased labor costs, and rising inflation. Economists/market participants recognize many cycles, one of which is the Kuznets cycle.

  In 2009, investors started to discover that such a cycle had been born in the form of the global initiative for infrastructure. Whether it's a country like India or China with new buildings and bridges to erect, or more developed countries with physical structures in need of a serious facelift, the Kuznets cycle appears to be alive and well for the foreseeable future.

  Again, the question is not whether to include commodities and companies that play a role in what some have called a $40 trillion initiative over the next 20 years. It is the specific routes by which to access these long-term trends, and the ability to add or reduce your position in them when inevitable minicycles occur within the larger Kuznets cycle that is important. It is also what will give you a chance to have your cake and eat it, too, as you might just meet or exceed the long-term returns of a buy-and-hold approach to these volatile areas, but with less frantic moments along the way.

The bottom line: taking account of business cycles, then applying careful risk-management discipline, is a powerful combination for long-term success in global growth investing.

- *Kondratiev wave or cycle (45–60 years): Named after Nikolai Kondratiev.* I know what you are thinking: Is Rob really going to talk about something that takes 45–60 years to occur? I may be gone by then. Fortunately, I only want to make mention of this longer-term cycle, as I think it does underlie the more relevant, investment-related cycles described earlier. Also, the "K-cycle" as it is also known, is made up of smaller periods known as "waves." There are three types: expansion, stagnation, and recession.

The phases of Kondratiev's waves also carry with them social shifts and changes in the public mood. The first stage of expansion and growth, the "spring" stage, encompasses a social shift in which the wealth, accumulation, and innovation that are present in this first period of the cycle create upheavals and displacements in society. Want a recent, real-life example of this? It has been widely reported in recent years that the magnitude of wealth disparity (i.e., rich vs. poor) in the United States reached unprecedented levels in the past decade. That is exactly what K-cycle theory anticipates.

That wealth disparity and the negative economic changes result in redefining employment. As we saw throughout 2008 and into 2009, jobs vanished and stories of underemployed and "discouraged" workers (those who were without a job for so long they stopped looking) made people adjust to the new employment environment. You may have heard of layoffs at a big business and were told that "those jobs are not coming back." Don't think this is the first time that has happened. After all, when they laid off people at the buggy whip factory a century ago, those jobs did not come back either.

In the next phase, the "summer" stagflation, there is a mood of affluence from the previous growth stage that changes the attitude towards work in society, creating inefficiencies. For instance, people who, 20 years ago, would take whatever job they could to combat the recession, might refuse to apply to CVS or McDonald's, feeling that despite their unemployed state, the job was now "beneath them." After all, they live in a nice house, with three flat-screens and a fancy car. They have tasted the other side of life and are not going back to what they consider to be the dark side.

After this stage comes the season of deflationary growth, or the plateau period. The popular mood changes during this period as well. It shifts toward stability, normalcy, and isolationism after the policies and economics during unpopular excesses of war. If this stays true to form, the U.S. economy will get back to growing, but slowly, and with consumers preferring to retain the frugal ways they suddenly found in 2009, following a disastrous period for all things financial. I was as shocked as anyone at how fast the savings rate shot up in the United States during 2009. It showed that, as a nation, we had it in us all the time but needed to be pushed to the brink to bring out that behavior. Regardless of how things develop over the next decade or two, this generation of investors now has a place in their mind for frugality that had been lost in the glamour of the 1980s and 1990s. Some will translate that into the need for a return to the kind of all-weather asset allocation approaches that worked before 1980, but many will not. That, unfortunately, could offset much of the economic progress made by the use of more contained spending habits.

Finally, the "winter" stage, that of severe depression, includes the integration of previous social shifts and changes into the social fabric of society, supported by the shifts in innovation and technology. We can only hope that during our lifetimes and our kids' and grandkids' lifetimes that we don't get to this wave in the cycle. There will be much debate years from now as to whether we did get there in 2008. After all, as the stock market sprang back up starting in March 2009, high joblessness rates persisted from Detroit to California to New York City. To bring the conversation of cycles full-circle (or full-cycle, if you will), we cannot control the cycles; they are much bigger than us. However, armed with this knowledge of how they work, we can take comfort in our ability to invest within the constraints and opportunities afforded by each type of cycle, and pursue the most successful outcome one can reasonably expect, regardless of what comes our way.

One key thought leader in the area of economic and market cycles is Michael A. Alexander. Ironically, he is not an investment manager or even a professional economist. According to his bio at the website for the books he has written on cycles (http://my. netlink.net/~malexan/STOCK_CYCLES.htm), he is a research engineer at a drug company. However, he "has a lifelong interest in economic and stock market history." His first book, *Stock Cycles*, published in November 2000 by iUniverse Star, was produced following five years of historical research and economic analysis. He has written three more books since then, and in my mind, he is one of the "go-to" sources for information on long-term cyclical investing. Here is an example of his thinking, explaining the value of his books, from that website:

> Stocks go up in the long run, so there's nothing to worry about, right? Between 2000 and 2002 the NASDAQ lost two thirds of its value. We are told to ignore short-term fluctuations. After all, stocks go up in the long run. So in a few years we will forget this nasty interlude, right? Stocks do go up in the long run— but only half the time. *Stock Cycles* covers 200 years of stock market history to show that stock returns are cyclical. Half the time, such as 1982–2000, the stock market moves strongly upward. The other half, like 1966–1982, stocks go nowhere for years. Based on P/R, a novel valuation model, it is likely that the market peak in 2000 was the beginning of the downside of the cycle, and that an index fund purchased at year 2000 levels will underperform money market funds for the next 20 years. The stock cycle is a consequence of the Kondratiev cycle. The Kondratiev cycle covers 800 years of economic history to show how this cycle is intimately involved in the evolution of the economic, political, and social trends of our time. Investing in a Secular Bear Market picks up where *Stock Cycles* left off and charts a course for the progress of the secular bear market that began in 2000.

In a March 16, 2001, article published on www.safehaven.com, Alexander displayed this very telling chart and described it. A decade later, you can see that he was right as rain!

There have been 14 secular trends since 1800: seven secular bull markets and seven secular bear markets. Table 9.1 shows a plot of the S&P 500 and its precursors on a constant-dollar basis over the past two centuries. The secular bull and bear markets have been marked on the figure.

The impact of secular trends on long-term investment performance is very great. To illustrate this, consider two investors, Mr. A and Mr. B. Mr. A is fully invested during the secular bear market periods whereas Mr. B is invested during the secular bull periods [see Table 9.1]. All transactions occur in January, so Mr. A buys a hypothetical index fund in January 1802 and sells it in January 1815. Mr. B buys the fund in January 1815 and sells in January 1835, at which point Mr. A buys again. This continues down until the present. The performance of the two investors is shown in [Table 9.1].

Note that despite being invested for nearly a century in lengthy chunks of time running from 8 to 20 years, Mr. A's overall return is less than 1 percent per year in real terms. Mr. B gains an average real return of 13 percent for his 103 years in the market.

It was the work of Mr. Alexander, along with many other "investment realists," that has, over the past decade or so, formed my thoughts on what works for investors. As you have seen in this book,

Table 9.1   200+ Years of Secular Bull and Bear Stock Markets

Mr. A (Secular Bear Markets)			Mr. B (Secular Bull Markets)		
Period	Duration	Annual Real Return	Period	Duration	Annual Real Return
1802–1815	13	+2.8%	1815–1835	20	+9.6%
1835–1843	8	−1.1%	1843–1853	10	+12.5%
1853–1861	8	−2.8%	1861–1881	20	+11.5%
1881–1896	15	+3.7%	1896–1906	10	+11.5%
1906–1921	15	−1.9%	1921–1929	8	+24.8%
1929–1949	20	+1.2%	1949–1966	17	+14.1%
1966–1982	16	−1.5%	1982–2000	18	+14.8%
Overall	95	+0.3%	Overall	103	+13.2%

the patterns of what works are very similar, regardless of whether you call yourself a "conservative" investor, a "moderate" or "aggressive," or anywhere in between. The only question is how to customize a combination of the approaches to your specific requirements, goals, and objectives. That is taken care of either on your own or with the help of a professional financial advisor. As you can tell by now, my investment team and I are here for you either way.

The Global Cycle Strategy in Action

For global cycle, we are typically looking 5 to 10 years out, on average. However, since that is an average, the concepts of all varieties of economic and market cycles explained earlier in this chapter are incorporated into the strategy.

The global cycle strategy is for the money people will not need for at least five years, and perhaps a half a generation or longer. For instance, China and India, which are two of the core themes of global cycle, are currently regarded as "emerging markets." Our belief is that in 20 years, they will simply be known as "markets," as they will have developed. These, along with our interest in global infrastructure, fall in line with the concept of the Kuznets cycle described earlier. However, some of the themes we invest in for global cycle will evolve faster, over two years, three years, five years, and so on. For instance, in late 2005, gold started an ascent from $400 an ounce to about triple that level by late 2009. While that story may or may not have several more chapters to go, what we witnessed there was something akin to a Kitchin Cycle. Interestingly, the dramatic ramp-up in demand for gold, and later the rise in the gold price, started for traditional reasons, but then had a second wind when exchange-traded funds (ETFs) dedicated to owning gold came along. Those ETFs and their buyers created a sort of self-fulfilling prophecy, in which gold demand was in part rooted in demand for the ETF, not for use of the gold for commercial or industrial purposes. This is an example of what I mean when I say that our job is not to endorse the reasons for why things occur. Our job is to evaluate the risk and reward of investing in it, and make businesspersons' decisions from that conclusion.

The global cycle strategy is an equity-focused style that takes a long-term view of the global economy and financial markets. It seeks to capitalize on secular themes identified by my research team and

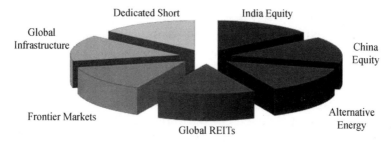

Figure 9.1   Sample Global Cycle Strategy Allocation

me. We are looking for situations where a long, positive business cycle is occurring or will develop. While usually we are looking for what to buy to participate in a secular trend, we also reserve the right to short a market segment that we think is in a death spiral. Given my comments on the state of the high-quality bond market after 30 years of falling interest rates, you can imagine that the idea of shorting long-term U.S. Treasury bonds (through mutual funds that do this) is certainly fair game for the global cycle strategy. To me, this is yet another example of the nearly limitless potential that exists within the strategic framework I have created.

In global cycle, we carefully select active equity fund managers who are focused on the specific secular themes chosen. As such, global cycle is a multitheme/multimanager portfolio. We actively manage the portfolio to rebalance the allocations and specific weightings assigned to each manager (see Figure 9.1).

The Global Cycle Investment Process

The goal is to construct a diversified portfolio of multiple secular themes that are actively managed by seasoned fund managers who have a competitive edge and unique level of expertise in their area of focus. The process begins by identifying global themes that are in the midst of a long, positive business cycle, as discussed at length earlier in this chapter. We are looking for those that seem to offer a favorable risk-reward scenario. We then identify and select an active fund manager who we believe best represents that theme. Quantitative analysis is applied to help determine fund weightings, and technical analysis is used to assist in determining buy and sell points.

Since some of these themes are in their early years of business development, there is potential for a considerable degree of volatility. Thus, I actively manage the portfolio and may increase or decrease its exposure to any given theme based on market conditions. I may also use short positions to hedge the portfolio and reduce potential volatility during periods of high perceived market risk. As you have come to know about me by now, the ability to short as needed, when needed, but without being compelled to do so all the time is a required element of everything I do as an investment strategist. The history of cycles described in this chapter should make a loud statement to you about why I am so passionate about that feature of the investment process.

Objectives of the Global Cycle Strategy

The desired result is a diversified, aggressive equity holding that:

- Pursues specific investment themes on a global scale
- Diversifies across multiple funds to reduce "single manager risk"
- Has the flexibility to hedge the portfolio, use cash, and hence deliver lower volatility and lower correlation to the broad markets than traditional "long-only" global equity strategies
- Generates superior risk-adjusted returns relative to other aggressive growth strategies

Risk Management.   Global cycle is an opportunistic portfolio that seeks to generate long-term capital growth, yet with the flexibility to hedge and assist in controlling its net long exposure. At the top level, risk is managed by the design and construction of its fund-of-funds approach. The portfolio will

- Diversify across multiple equity themes and managers, each of whom focuses on a different discipline.
- Buy short-index securities as a hedge.
- Adjust cash levels as needed and may use cash defensively.
- Employ an ongoing due-diligence process that includes actively monitoring the managers. This includes a strict sell discipline for all the managers employed. Reasons for termination may include the following:
  - A fund has become too large.
  - A fund company has become too "institutionalized."

- Turnover and/or material personnel changes on the investment team.
- A fund has exhibited style drift.
- Lagging performance for unexplainable reasons.
- The investment thesis was wrong.

Portfolio Positioning. Global cycle provides financial advisors and their investors with an attractive equity holding that pursues a higher-risk/higher-reward approach, and one that can make a valuable addition to strategies that are managed with more conservative and more moderate risk/reward characteristics. It diversifies across multiple global equity managers, yet unlike traditional long-only strategies, it has the flexibility to hedge the portfolio and/or use cash liberally. Global cycle can be used as an attractive alternative to global equity strategies, global balanced strategies, aggressive allocation strategies, global macro hedge funds, and target-date funds (long term).

ETFs are sometimes used as a substitute or complement to mutual funds in global cycle portfolios. ETFs receive greater consideration for the global cycle strategy than either hybrid or concentrated equity do. Since global cycle is, at the broad level, an attempt to capitalize on long-term themes, we can access many of our investable themes through ETFs. The advantage is a lower internal cost to the portfolio, as ETFs tend to have lower expense ratios than traditional mutual funds. The other side of the story is that many areas in which we may choose to invest do not have an ETF that is truly a surrogate for the theme we want to invest in. Or the ETFs available come with ''hair'' on them, such as special tax treatment, lack of liquidity, and other concerns.

The main reason I tend to use more mutual funds than ETFs in this strategy is a simple assumption I make about reward and risk. I think that in this type of investing, active management is extremely valuable. When it comes to investing in China, frontier markets, or biotech, I want ''go-to'' fund managers who have their hands on the pulse of what is driving that particular theme over the long run. Then, I want to oustsource the day-to-day decision making within those style areas to experienced managers who are entrenched there, and get their input on how market conditions are impacting their portfolio. It is this regular exchange of knowledge and access to specialized talent around the world that excites me about what global cycle has become. ETFs will continue to play a role here, but my primary concern is looking for managers who run mutual funds and are accessible to our team for us to provide meaningful ongoing due diligence on them.

Benchmarking the Performance of the Global Cycle Allocation Strategy

As you now know, global cycle portfolios are not bound by geographic region. I am looking for the best long-term trends. It is possible that at some point, all will be in the United States or all will be found outside the United States. It is also possible that at some point, the thematic focus will emphasize fixed income and commodities, alongside the equity funds we own. Neither scenario is likely, so the obvious choice is to benchmark global cycle against a global equity index. The MSCI World Free Index is the most recognized benchmark of that type, and so it is the primary benchmark for global cycle. And since we know investors are always curious about how any growth investment performs against the S&P 500, we use that as a secondary benchmark when we report returns for global cycle portfolios.

PART IV

YOU'VE COME THIS FAR, NOW SCORE! (PUTTING THE STRATEGY TO WORK)

14

YOU'VE COME THIS FAR...
NOW SCORE! (PUTTING THE
STRATEGY TO WORK)

10

Evaluating Your Performance—the Right Way

I have tried to expand the boundaries of investment education for all who come in contact with my firm and me. We certainly don't know it all, but we do feel our disdain for conventional wisdom and our nontraditional investment approach allows us to have some insights that are not widely disseminated to the investment public and much of our industry.

I have always approached investing in general as a process of meeting life's financial obligations, as opposed to beating a standard stock or bond "benchmark." That does not mean you shouldn't compare yourself to some investment index for an indication of how you are doing. It just means that you should not get obsessed with comparisons to inanimate objects (benchmarks) that don't know you, don't care about you, and are not going to change the way you live your life—unless you fall prey to their charms as much of the financial media does.

I am confident in my belief that benchmark envy is one of the most destructive forces to investors. And I am equally confident that it will continue to be. Let's be realistic: people love to keep score. That's what benchmarking is. And the same sociological factors that help market pundits on television get ratings also account for the overarching obsession with how one is doing against "the market" or whatever benchmark they use. Again, benchmarking is useful, but it's the context that people get wrong.

Benchmarks, as I see them, are meant to be used for comparison over long stretches of time—5 to 10 years, maybe three in some cases. However, I have seen way too many cases in which investment decisions were made following short-term observations of an investment versus a benchmark, which caused the investor, advisor, or both to conclude that the investment was "not working out."

This chapter deals with performance measurement. Each section of this chapter takes a different performance evaluation concept or statistic and attempts to describe it in a way that you and I can understand. What drives the calculations of these statistics is complex, but understanding what they mean to you in the "real world" is all most investors are concerned with (and rightly so). By reading this chapter, do-it-yourself investors will greatly increase their awareness of how to truly identify whether their portfolio is working for them or if they are holding a ticking time bomb, masked by good raw performance that, adjusted for risk, is more dangerous than they realize.

Advisors, by reading this chapter, will have a convenient resource to explain these sometimes complex and frequently misunderstood evaluation tools to their clients. I have found that when you demystify performance measurement for investors, they truly appreciate what they are getting out of their portfolio. It allows expectations to be met for both parties, and promotes the "teammates, not opponents" idea I feel is so important in cases when an investor seeks the help of a professional financial advisor.

Capturing Investment Success

Earlier in this book you saw how market environments vary greatly from period to period. I'm not talking about days or weeks, but rather a series of months and years. Now we'll dissect the latter half of that 100+-year period in a different way, to illustrate a very helpful way to analyze your portfolio's return.

Using monthly return data from Yahoo! Finance on the S&P 500 Index back to 1950, I noticed that the frequency of positive monthly returns for the index could be very different from one investment era to the next. Table 10.1 shows different periods of time, and the percentage of months in that period in which the S&P went up. I've added a short description of each period to remind you what was going on in the world and markets at the time:

Table 10.1 Frequency of Positive Months for the S&P 500 over Various Time Periods

Years	% Up	Events
1950–1960	56%	Post–World War II, the United States takes a leadership role in the world
1960–1965	64%	"Camelot" (Kennedy administration) and eventually the start of the Vietnam War
1965–1982	51%	A long, difficult secular bear market for stocks; recession, war, and social unrest
1982–1990	59%	The start of the biggest economic expansion in decades (and the bubbles that followed)
1990–2000	71%	The era in which investing went mainstream and Wall Street rode high; tech was king
2000–2003	37%	The bubble bursts; 40%+ losses in major stock indexes over three years
2003–2008	68%	"Bubble—part 2": Markets rise without a major decline.
2008–2009	50%	The "crash" and the "bounce"

Now let's look a bit closer. The 1950s were a period of solid market gains. The 1960s started fine, but eventually we entered the worst extended period in modern market history. During the 1965–1982 bear market, the S&P 500 went up only six months out of each year, on average. As a result, market returns were near zero, and that's before the impact of inflation, which was at a very high level in the 1970s. As you can tell, if the stock market goes up only half of the time (in terms of months), making a reasonable profit is very difficult.

The remainder of the 1980s showed a higher trend, except for the short period around the1987 crash. Still, monthly returns moved back to the range where solid profits could be made.

When you see the 1990s on this chart, it gives you an idea of just how "easy" that decade was in investment history. Let's face it, if your monthly statement is up in 7 out of every 10 months, you feel like a genius. But too many people got used to that feeling, so when the bubble burst in early 2000, they were caught completely unprepared. All of a sudden, your monthly statement was negative most of the time. That is why we heard many say back then that they did not even open their statements for months. Many investors assumed that the market going up 70 percent of the time was "normal" and to be expected. Unfortunately, this is still part of the psyche of many market participants.

During the bubble's encore from 2003 to 2007, the market rose over two thirds of the time, and that feeling of complacency came back. We have often heard it said by people in our industry that "the stock market goes up 70 percent of the time," and this is the justification for the buy-and-hold strategies that pervade the industry. Our look at the last 57 years shows us that the 70 percent figure is an exception, not the rule. Different market environments have very different impacts on the same portfolio.

Now that we have debunked the oft-told fairytale that the stock market goes up 70 percent of the time, we'll look at another critical factor in how a portfolio performs—capture ratio.

"Capture Ratio": What Is It, and How Does It Help You?

Capture ratio is a statistic that tells you how much of the market's move you have experienced. The "market" can be any index you can plug into the analytical software, but since the S&P 500 stock index is Morningstar's standard stock market benchmark, we'll use that example for now.

If for every 10 percent up move in the market your portfolio grew by 8 percent, your capture ratio is 80 percent. Capture ratio is often expressed as a decimal, so an 80 percent capture ratio might show up on a research report as "0.80." Since we are talking about a time period when the market went up, we call this an *up capture ratio*, the portion of the up market that you capture. It works the same way on the downside. If the market went down 10 percent, and your portfolio went down 6 percent, you would have a *down capture ratio* of 60 percent. The problem for many investors is that, unbeknownst to them, they have a portfolio whose down capture ratio is near 100 percent. That can cause nasty surprises.

Capture ratios can be negative, too. Note that I said the down capture was 60 percent, not –60 percent. A negative down capture ratio can be a very good thing, since it means you have made money in a down market. So, if you made a 2 percent gain when the market fell 10 percent, your down capture ratio is −0.20 or −20 percent.

The most common place you'd find a negative down capture is in an investment that is dedicated to shorting the market (so-called bear funds) or some segment of it. Of course, such investments would not be expected to produce a strong up capture (in fact, it would likely be negative, as a bear fund will likely lose money in an up stock market, as it is designed to profit only from bad times. I'll have more on this later in the book).

Capture Ratios—A Simple Example

If someone handed you $1,000 a day for seven days in a row, then made you give back $1,000 for each of the next three days, you'd still be way ahead. In fact, if this happened for a full year, you'd be $146,000 ahead by the end of the year. That's a nice second income just for showing up! This is a game you'd like to play next year and every year.

What if the next year, without warning, the game changed? The same person handed you $1,000 a day for four straight days. However, this year, you are forced to give back $1,000 for days 5 through 10 of each 10-day cycle. That is, you no longer win 70 percent of the time. Rather, you win just 40 percent of the time. You are not $4,000 ahead as you were at the end of each cycle last year; you are $2,000 behind! This continues for the entire year, and you end the year with $73,000 less than when you started. Ugh! You think to yourself, "I'm not playing this game anymore!"

This example combined two key factors every investor should know before setting their performance expectations:

1. What are my expected capture ratios?
2. If those capture ratios continue into the future (and there's no guarantee of that, but it's better than not knowing anything about your portfolio), how might my portfolio to react to different market conditions?

We showed in this example how a traditional portfolio (many of which have up and down capture ratios near 100 percent) performs very differently in different market environments (recall that there have been periods where the market goes up 70 percent of the time and others where it's up only about 40 percent of the time). Now, this may not be news to you, but what you should know is that there are better approaches than "buy and hope." Sometimes the notes change, and you must be flexible enough to adapt.

Bottom line: there will be good markets and bad markets. Since predicting the future is not anyone's best talent (especially economists and weather people), knowing how much of the ups and downs may be "captured" by your portfolio leaves you much better prepared to navigate the markets as a long-term investor.

Consistency Counts (If You're Into That Sort of Thing)

Some investors emphasize reward over risk. Others do the opposite. Most have a tradeoff somewhere in the middle. In nonindustry terms, some are okay with a bumpy road on the way to their eventual destination, because their car can ramp up to high speeds. But it also can break down sometimes, and that may keep them from reaching their destination as soon as they would like. The flip side is that they may get there very quickly, and that is the motivation that overrules everything. They trade consistency in their returns for a higher return in good markets. In industry terms, this is what we call a "high standard deviation" investor or portfolio manager. I will coin the phrase "HSD" for short.

Others drive more slowly, because getting to the destination quickly takes a back seat (oh, awful pun in a driving example!) to the primary goal . . . to indeed get there. They emphasize minimizing the chance of the car breaking down along the way. They also may need to put higher-quality gasoline in the car, and that costs more (i.e., their investment cost to get that smoother ride is somewhat higher) than the HSD investor's gasoline costs. This passenger's car has very good shock absorbers, and will start to rattle at very high speeds. All of this is part of their priority, which is a smoother ride than the HSD investor is likely to endure. While I may ruffle some feathers or simply bring back some memories for some people (not yours truly, I assure you), we'll call this other type of investor, who seeks consistency first, then as much as they can make given that constraint, a low standard deviation investor. For short, we'll call them . . . wait for it . . . LSD investors and portfolio managers.

The explanation above has a clear, vital purpose: to get you to understand in real-world terms and to think about the concept of Standard Deviation in your portfolio. Hopefully my car-driving analogy "drove home" the point. Just in case, here is how www. businessdictionary.com defines an investment's Standard Deviation: "the variability (volatility) of a security, derived from the security's historical returns, and used in determining the range of possible future returns. The higher the standard deviation, the greater the potential for volatility." **Standard Deviation is really all about consistency and predictability of one's range of returns in various market conditions**.

Standard Deviation is perhaps the most common measure of investment "risk" used by the investment advisory business. You have likely seen a four-quadrant graph of an investment's historical "return" on the horizontal axis and "risk" on the vertical axis. The return figure shown would be the investment's actual return (typically annualized) over whatever period of time the graph covers. The "risk" figure used is most commonly the Standard Deviation of the investment over that same time period. I suspect this is because Standard Deviation is measured consistently regardless of what type of investment style or security you are analyzing. It is calculated simply by averaging the historical returns and figuring out the average ("standard") distance ("deviation") from that average. To me, "risk" is best defined by using some other measure of volatility, such as Downside Capture Ratio (e-mail me if you are not familiar with that term) or maybe Beta. However, those are measured against an index, so it is more difficult to standardize the presentation of them.

Consider the market's manic behavior in both directions from September 2007 through April 2010. We saw the S&P 500 double on two separate occasions, and also lose at least half of its value on two other occasions. As I write this, we are in the midst of a rally that has advanced about 75 percent off the lows of 13 months ago. The most important question any investor or financial advisor should ask themselves (preferably in front of the mirror) right now is, "Am I an HSD or an LSD investor?" If you are somewhere in between, you better figure out where on the HSD/LSD spectrum you are. If you don't, then you have a high risk of disappointment, either from jealousy in roaring, stimulus-propelled up markets, or from heartbreak during vicious, unrelenting declines. Even if volatility were tame for a long time and markets were friendly, you will be glad that at least you figured out who you are as an investor. After all, reducing the possibility of disappointment also reduces the likelihood of emotional or erratic investment decisions. Besides, it's nice to know who you really are . . .

Using Rolling Returns for Better Analysis

Let's continue with a discussion of rolling returns. I firmly believe that this is a better way to truly evaluate a manager's past effectiveness than simply looking at trailing returns (past one, three, five years) or annual returns (performance for each calendar year). These are arbitrary periods, created by database companies. They are certainly not useless, but used in isolation, they can be among the most misleading statistics you can find to size up an investment manager (see Table 10.2).

Let's Play a Performance Analysis Game

Take a close look at Table 10.2, which contains annual percentage returns of three investments. Now, let's play a short game. Assume that you are going to choose one of these investments for the majority of your portfolio. You know nothing else about the investments, so you have no choice but to base your decision on their performance over the past five years. Since past performance is not necessarily a guide to future performance, I trust you will never actually try to limit yourself like this in real life. Okay, with that disclaimer out of the way, let's go back to our game.

Which would you choose, and why? To help you decide, here is a quick analysis, based simply on the numbers you see in the table:

Table 10.2 Annual Returns of Three Different Hypothetical Portfolios

	A	B	C
2003	−23.0	24.4	0.3
2004	34.6	13.9	19.1
2005	6.2	12.3	6.3
2006	10.4	10.8	8.6
2007	14.5	16.4	20.6

Investment A has been the most volatile, and showed the potential to post big losses as in 2003. It also had the highest single-year return.

Investment B has been the steadiest of the three, reaching double digits each year.

Investment C has managed a gain each year, but has returned over 10 percent only twice in the five-year period.

Now it is time to make a decision. Which one would you pick, and why?

Now that you have answered, here is an interesting fact that you may not have realized. All of these investments are the same. They are all one-year returns for the S&P 500 Stock Index. What?! How can that be? The returns are completely different! Okay, let me explain.

Investment A is the return of the S&P 500 from February to January of each year, starting in February of 2002 and ending in January of 2007. For instance, A's return for 2003 is the year ending January 31, 2003. Investment B is the return of the S&P 500 from October 2002 to September 2007. Investment C is the return of the S&P 500 from July 2002 to June 2007.

In other words, depending on which month in 2002 you started your investment, the returns from one anniversary of that investment to the next may be completely different. Put another way, there are 12 different "annual" returns each year for any index, fund, stock, and so on. Given the obsession by the media and many investors with analyzing returns only by full calendar years (i.e., January 1 to December 31 of any given year), you could say that you are only getting one twelfth of the information you need to analyze an investment's past returns!

A table or graph that shows each of the 12-month returns (February–January, March–February, April–March, etc.) is referred to as an analysis of *rolling returns*. In this example, it's a 12-month rolling return analysis we are talking about. Depending on how high-powered your analytics tool is, you can run rolling return analysis for 3-month, 6-month, 5-year, 10-year, or any other period. In each case you are looking at many different overlapping periods, not one complete period followed by the next complete period.

More importantly, if you did have this information available to you, how would it help you? Particularly if you see rolling returns in a graph, you can quickly see the tendencies of an investment to reach returns of different levels. One thing I look for in any mutual fund I buy is how often its rolling 12-month return has crossed into negative territory and for how long. That is much more meaningful than some static performance period that a database company created out of convenience.

Unfortunately, what Morningstar and other companies did, unintentionally, is focus everyone on the same limited number of time periods to evaluate the performance of mutual funds and other managed investments. Is there something magical and vital about how a fund did over a 1-, 3-, 5-, or 10-year period? Perhaps there is but what about the dozens of performance periods in between? This is a particularly important issue when the markets are volatile, as they were in 2008 and 2009. Simply sliding the performance date range one or two months in either direction could give you a completely different picture. For example, given the volatility of late 2008 and early 2009, a fund's three-year return, as well as its ranking within its peer group, from September 30, 2005, to September 30, 2008, could be entirely different than its three-year return from October 31, 2005, to October 31, 2008. I prefer to use both rolling periods, and what we call *peak-to-trough analysis*, whereby we analyze returns from different market tops to market bottoms, and vice versa. We even have something we call a *bull-bear analysis* we do on our own portfolios and on individual funds we follow.

If the stock and bond markets gyrate up and down and an investment shows a historical ability to not gyrate with it, that is one very positive point about the investment (of course, it is only one part of the analysis). To summarize, a rolling return graph helps you characterize an investment's historical nature as slow and steady, hit or miss, or something else.

It is a shame that the investment advisory industry does not place more emphasis on rolling returns. Given the more even mix of up and down markets during this decade as compared to the 1980s and 1990s (which were dominated by positive returns in all major stock and bond indexes), I hope this will change.

There is no law in investing that says you stop analyzing past performance after you have checked the calendar-year returns and returns over trailing periods (past three years, past five years, etc.). Rolling returns, if you can get performance data in that format, are even more valuable than all of that.

Don't Let the Market Be Your Evil Twin (R-Squared)

So, now we have learned that it is easy to be fooled by your own portfolio's performance. What seems like a great investment can turn out to be a bull market hero and bear market goat. Rather than continue with the animal analogies, let's move on to an important, related concept that will further help you decipher what you own.

Your portfolio may have done well in the good times. It mimicked the market on the way up. It fooled you into thinking it is your buddy, like a twin sibling who will always be there for you. But it is only now, when the going gets tough (and who knows for how long?), that your twin turns evil. Whatever trouble it gets itself into, it drags you into the mess. To help you understand how your portfolio can be "influenced" by the market, there is a simple concept with a funky name: R-squared.

The fancy statistic for this is called *R-squared*, and it answers the question of how much of your portfolio's return was due to the movement of the market, and not the manager's particular skills. Recall a discussion earlier in this book about how people were so impressed by the returns of money managers in the bull market, only to find out that the same managers could be just as bad as a bear market. These investors learned the hard way that the market, not the managers' brains, was driving the returns in good and bad market environments. There's an old Wall Street saying that one should not "confuse genius with a bull market." I think you get the picture.

I tried several Internet sources to get a definition of R-squared that I was comfortable with. Since I don't speak "geek" as well as I used to, it was tough. Investopedia.com saved me. It defines R-squared as "a statistical measure that represents the percentage of a fund or security's movements that can be explained by movements in a benchmark index. For fixed-income securities, the benchmark is the T-bill. For equities, the benchmark is the S&P 500." So this is like asking your portfolio how much it likes to mimic what the market (benchmark) is doing.

Investopedia goes on to say that:

> R-squared values range from 0 to 100. 100 means that all move-
> ments of a security are completely explained by movements in
> the index. Between 85 and 100 indicates the fund's perform-
> ance patterns have been in line with the index. A fund with a
> low R-squared (70 or less) doesn't act much like the index.

So R-squared tells us to what degree the market is influencing
your portfolio in good times and bad. You may also ask, "If my portfolio's R-squared is 90, I know that means that the market is 90 percent of the reason my portfolio does what it does. But what is
influencing the other one tenth of my return?" The answer is
"everything else"—factors other than the market itself, such as the
skill of the manager and the investment style used. Note also that R-
squared should be evaluated over at least a three-year period so that
you have enough data for the number to be reliable.

Historically, many equity investment styles have tended to have
very high R-squared readings. In other words, those categories of
investing often fail to succeed without a lot of help from the broad
stock market. That often implies that when the market goes south as
it did in 2008, those equity approaches do not do a good job of
shielding you from the damage. We only need to look to investment
style returns in 2008 to see this. It was a blowout. You may ask, since
an S&P Index fund has a 100 percent R-squared, are the stock categories that occupy the typical investor's portfolio really doing
enough to differentiate themselves? Is there any originality out
there? Is simply diversifying among different types of stocks a real
solution for mixed market conditions? The answer to all of these
questions appears to be no.

Unfortunately, there are billions of dollars invested in actively
managed, professionally managed stock portfolios that have R-
squared of over 90. That means that less than one tenth of the return produced by the manager has anything to do with the manager's skill; the market's movement is the real reason the performance
is what it is. One of my favorite sayings is, "There are some things in
life you can control and some you can't." I think that recognizing
this is one of the grand keys to getting what you want out of life.

I know this: if you are paying management fees expecting to get
outstanding manager skill at your disposal and come to realize that

their skill is not much of a factor, you *can* control that. You can stop paying for mediocre performance! Then your only decision is whether to pay less for market-driven performance (via an index or index-like strategy), or search for managers whose performance tends to be more a result of their own work, and not the whims of the market. This last point is what I have devoted a good portion of my career to researching and discovering for clients.

For the actual data on R-squared and the other statistics covered in this chapter, I suggest you go to Morningstar.com or one of that firm's professional database products, which divides the mutual fund universe into about 80 different categories.

Now it is time to conclude this book with Chapter 11. I am not talking about the kind that signifies protection from your creditors, though one goal of the book is to put you in a financial position where that will never be a realistic possibility in your lifetime or that of your children and grandkids. The goal of Chapter 11 of this book is to leave you with some parting wisdom to carry forward into the rest of your days as an investor.

11

Putting It All Together

CHINESE FOOD AND ASSET ALLOCATION—
PERFECT TOGETHER!

Tom Keane was the governor of my home state of New Jersey during most of the 1980s. I remember that he did a series of commercials promoting the state as a tourist site. The tagline of the commercials was "New Jersey and you—perfect together." When I moved to Florida in 1997, there were three things my wife and I found we could not replace from our days in the New York area: pizza, bagels, and Chinese food. It is just not the same outside of the New York–New Jersey area. I cannot explain why.

Fortunately, some local Florida establishments have bridged the gap on the pizza and bagels. But Chinese food is the one that still leave us yearning for what we had up north. My mind working as it does, I naturally found an analogy between Chinese food, as it is served in the United States, and the concept of asset allocation. At this point, you are either very hungry or your stomach is turning from that attempted analogy. Either way, I have mentioned this to several financial advisors, and they agree that it makes sense to them.

Here is what I mean: when you go to a Chinese restaurant, whether you are taking out as we did traditionally on Sunday nights in New Jersey, or eating in, your meal is served as follows: you get a big container of white rice, which you are supposed to line your plate with. That serves as the base for your meal. Next, you take out of the container the type of food you want to be your main dish.

Often, this is a combination of two or more different dishes. You take what you want and put it on top of the bed of white rice, and you are all set. Note that I left off any mention of egg rolls, spring rolls, wonton/egg drop/hot-and-sour soup, and spare ribs, to avoid confusion. Those are appetizers in my book, and we are talking about the "main course" of Chinese f . . . uh . . . asset allocation.

As I mentioned, you can top that plate of white rice with any number of dishes. Some will be light, others pungent, and some may be very spicy. If you add tofu and vegetables to your rice, you will have a bland meal, but your stomach will probably be fine later that night. If you add the ultra-spicy eggplant or beef dish, your taste buds may thank you, but there is a risk that there will be, shall we say, bumps in the road to happiness along the way. That is the crux of the analogy to asset allocation using these strategies.

The hybrid strategy represents the white rice on your plate. It serves as a nice base for a portfolio, and goes with nearly any combination of investment "flavors" you wish to add. Concentrated equity is sort of like adding chicken with cashew nuts in a brown sauce to that white rice. Not too spicy, contains familiar flavors, but when done right, it's a real winner. Finally, global cycle is a more spicy dish, but one that offers a fantastic taste experience—and is less likely to cause heartburn than a lot of dishes you could add to that plain white rice.

If you are like me, you probably want to take a break from reading this book and go for some takeout—but resist the urge, we are almost at the finish line. And the next time you get to the New York area, I don't have to tell you where to stop for lunch!

Mixing the Strategies—without Food Analogies

The concept of "core and explore" is familiar to many financial advisors and investors. The idea is to choose a portfolio style that represents your primary way of thinking about investing, and make it the biggest portion of your portfolio. That's your core. The explore portion is what is left. It allows you to take a smaller part of your wealth and direct it toward the pursuit of a different reward-risk combination than your core portfolio may allow. I will now provide some examples of this for different investor types. It is critical not to confuse this with investment advice! These are simply guidelines, not absolutes. Any specific combination of investment styles into a portfolio should either be done at your own discretion or with the help of a financial advisor. Still, as the creator of all of this, I feel it is helpful to start you down that path.

I will include up to four possible "elements" in the mix. Namely:

1. The hybrid strategy
2. The concentrated equity strategy
3. The global cycle strategy
4. A "floating mix" of two or all of the strategies

While each of the three strategies is dedicated to one of the three asset allocation styles, element 4 assumes that the three can be combined in a single account and allocated in a more tactical manner, if needed. More importantly for this exercise, it allows you to choose a floating allocation option alongside one or more of the other strategies. This takes the idea of investment flexibility, already central to each of the three strategies, and adds another dimension to it (see Figures 11.1 and 11.2).

Note that none of this should be confused with "market timing." There is nothing in my catalog of strategic investing moves that says "go to cash 100 percent" or "go all in," as they say in poker. I am talking about adjustments that are made with regard to risk *and* reward, not one or the other.

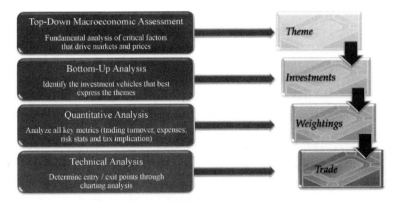

Figure 11.1   Constructing Asset Allocation Portfolios

Figure 11.2   Manager Due Diligence—an Ongoing Process

The Golden Ticket for the Next Decade and Beyond

Unlike young Charlie in the Willie Wonka movie, I don't believe investors will need a lucky break to succeed in the future. However, investment strategies for the twenty-first century must be more flexible, more thoughtful, and less tied to the performance of market indexes. For years now, the trend in my asset allocation approach has been away from the "usual suspects" in money management.

For the most part, these behemoth companies managing many billions of dollars in plain vanilla investment styles are investment dinosaurs. In my opinion, the investment returns of the future will be created by managers whose mandates include hedging techniques using short positions and/or options and futures, or those who don't base their decisions on how their portfolios are set up versus a market benchmark.

Buying and holding forever worked in the 1980s and 1990s. It ruined you in the late 1960s and throughout the 1970s. Do you want to take the chance that you invest for many years just to come up with nothing? A passive buy-and-hold-forever strategy does not employ the flexibility that today's global, nearly 24/7 markets will require. Asset allocation in its traditional form is extinct. Large cap vs. small cap vs. international has gone the way of the *Tyrannosaurus rex*.

Here's what I have learned: investors care about results and how logical the approach was to achieve the results! They also want to understand how the results were generated, so they can gauge for themselves if their managers and advisors were good or just lucky.

I don't think that investment industry people have ever worked harder to stay on top of what impacts the wealth their clients entrust to their guidance. They feel betrayed by the markets and some of their unscrupulous colleagues in the business, who have given the industry as a whole a bad name. They came out of 2008 with a chip on their shoulder—and that's a good thing for their clients.

From my conversations with dozens of financial planners before, during, and since 2008, I believe that most of them have a level of determination they have not had in the past. They are angry about what happened to their clients and their businesses, they are retooling and rethinking much of the conventional wisdom that guided them in the past, and they are taking concerted action to be truly capable leaders for their loyal clients and to attract additional ones. It is for them, their clients and the many individual investors that have chosen to play both roles (i.e., the serious do-it-yourself investor) that this book was written.

My job is to continuously search for ways to get these advisors and their clients to their goals, regardless of whether the stock market makes it easy (like it did in the 1980s and 1990s). We are not magicians, but we have experience and perspective. And you, by reading this book, obviously possess the patience and willingness to be educated. I don't know where that will get you in the next few days, weeks, or months. But, by using the principles, discipline, and approach contained in this book, I am confident that when it's time for you to use the money you've worked hard to earn, you will have accomplished what you set out to do. My team and I relish our "role-player" status on behalf of financial advisors and nonprofessional investors.

My responsibilities as an investment strategist do *not* include rooting for the stock market to go up. I am an investment professional, not a cheerleader. I don't know when the bears will tire and the bulls will take over again, or vice versa. I know it will happen, but there's no sense planning your portfolio around such events. With few exceptions, pure market timing (moving totally in or totally out of the market at once) is a loser's game. What is far more critical is to assess how a variety of market conditions may impact investors' ability to eventually reach their goals.

It is difficult to see that monthly statement yoyo up and down each month. Let's face it—people work hard to earn this money; it's annoying to give it back—ever. I understand this, but I also emphasize that this is the nature of investing for growth. As studies and recent scandals have shown, it's usually feast or famine; there's no such thing as a "steady" 10 percent return. You get there by muddling through the bear markets, keeping your overall portfolio volatility below that of the market, and resisting the temptation to make major, across-the-portfolio timing decisions, so that you're there when the bull charges.

As I've said before, even long secular bear markets create pockets of "bullish" opportunity that last months or even years. However, if you thought that your investment horizon was longer than it actually is, and/or your tolerance for price declines is lower than you once thought, that's a cause for action—the sooner the better.

I believe that for most people, investment success is about getting what they want out of their money, not about beating a market index. Thus, most investors can benefit from allocating a portion of their funds to lower-volatility strategies such as those described herein.

However, I view investing in high-quality bonds very differently from much of the advisory industry. To me, bonds issued by the U.S. government, its agencies, and high-quality U.S. corporations and municipalities are *not* a vehicle to use in pursuit of total return. They are best used for pure preservation of capital and predictable cash flow only.

Chasing Tails: How to Play Defense against a "Market Event"

If you remember everything you ever learned about "bell curves" and "normal distributions" in statistics class, good for you. But if you are like most of us who don't, here is what we believe is the most important thing an investor needs to know about determining the risk of a particular scenario's occurring: the ones that hurt the most are the ones that are least likely to happen—and then they do!

Perhaps you've become familiar with the metaphors "black swan," "100-year flood" and other references to rare events, such as huge moves in the stock market. In statistical jargon, events like this are the "tails" of that bell curve—the skinny fragments at the end of the graph that represent things that happen infrequently, but they do happen.

One could argue that from 2007 through 2009, we saw two "tail" events. From October 2007 through early March 2009, the S&P 500 Stock Index fell over 50 percent. Then, from that point in March through the end of 2009, that same index surged about 65 percent. As you now know, a tail event can be a very positive outcome or a very negative one. However, it is vital to understand that they can *both* be very dangerous to one's investment psyche, as well as to the portfolio.

Where I live in South Florida, we have learned all about hurricanes. One thing we learned the hard way this decade is that sometimes major storms come in bunches; that is, multiple major hurricanes occur in the same year or within a couple of years. We think the possibility that this type of scenario could occur in the global equity markets is far from remote. In fact, if you look at the period from 1960 to 1980, there were, according to data we sourced from stockcharts.com on the Dow Jones Industrial Average (the S&P 500 did not exist prior to 1970), several major market moves (of greater than 20 percent, though often much more), both up and down. We counted six up and five down. Compare that to the decades of the 1980s and 1990s, in which many of today's investors and financial advisors learned about investing. During that period, we counted five up moves and only two down moves of at least 20 percent.

"Gray Investing" Is Better Than "Black-and-White" Investing

Investing is not about doing only this or only that. In other words, it's not black and white. Your portfolio at any moment in time should account for risk and reward not separately, but simultaneously. I refer to this as investing always as some "shade of gray."

Growing your wealth successfully may require you to take on a different mind-set at different times. Putting all of your chips on "buy-and-hold" investing or "tactical asset allocation" can leave you very disappointed, and perhaps feeling as if you are always a step behind—because you are. Like everything in investing, it's an educated guess, but I feel that taking a "black-or-white" approach to anything in portfolio management today is a mistake.

Tail risk is something that every financial advisor had better have accounted for in the design of their client portfolios. If you were "kind of conservative" when the stock market crashed in 1987, or Iraq invaded Kuwait in 1990, or the Long-Term Capital hedge fund crisis suddenly roiled the markets, was that good enough? Or, do you need a consistently applied mechanism in your investment process that both recognizes the existence of tail events, and allows you to specifically designate a portion of your portfolio toward protecting against tail events?

So, don't end up like the dog that constantly chases its tail. Address tail risk, be resourceful about how to combat it, and keep searching for the next great idea to mix into your existing portfolio.

Market History: Know It and Learn from It

The 1980–2000 time period was not merely the most unrelenting rise in stock prices we've seen in the past century; it was the only one! Large market swings are a bigger part of history than most of today's investors realize. If you simply recognize and acknowledge that the stock market's character is not what most people think it is, and set your strategy to accommodate that, you open the door to an ocean of opportunity. At the same time, you can in turn potentially use the stock market as a long-term risk-reduction tool!

However, if you ignore the implications of this, it could be a long, depressing, worrisome, and frustrating trip from today to your ultimate financial outcome (note I did not say that outcome was a successful one). We are optimistic that as time goes on, a greater portion of the professional investment community and media will turn from bashing long-short mutual funds and fixating on investment fees and style purity to an understanding of exactly what we are talking about here: the stock market is a tool you use to achieve your intermediate- and long-term lifestyle objectives. Setting up a portfolio is not supposed to be like joining a cult, where you commit yourself to an inflexible philosophy for the rest of your life.

The other striking conclusion from this: most investors are putting *way* too much thought, energy, and emotion into what is happening in the stock market at the current time. Investing is not about living in the moment. Unless your time horizon is a week from next Thursday, you truly need to step back and do these five things:

1. Figure out what you want in life/lifestyle from the potential long-term success of your investment portfolio.
2. Think about over what period you hope and expect to start to reach your financial milestones.
3. Determine to what extent you are willing to risk the achievement of your goals by betting that the next many years will be more like the 1980s and 1990s than the rest of the twentieth (and start of the twenty-first) century.
4. Do your homework to figure out what comfortable, sensible alternatives are available to the mainstream approaches to protecting and growing wealth. Those approaches have let many people down.
5. Keep learning, keep seeking a better way to do this—or find someone who does it for you.

From Boring to Number One in 20 Weeks!

Building a successful football team is somewhat of a metaphor for several concepts in this book. So, why not close it out with one final investment-football analogy. One National Football League (NFL) season that was memorable to me for many reasons was the 1986 campaign. I had just started my business career after graduating from college and had spent the past few summers working as a pretzel vendor at Giants Stadium. The 1986 New York Giants allow me to describe one final important point for investors and investment advisors about keeping patient and waiting for your chance to allow your portfolio to reach its potential.

So, consider the season of the 1986 New York Giants (often referred to as the "football Giants" even though the Giants baseball team moved from New York to San Francisco over 50 years ago).

The Giants at that time were lovable losers, having endured many horrible seasons in the 1970s and early 1980s, yet selling out every game—and with a waiting list for season tickets in the tens of thousands. The Giants team of 1986 started with revived hopes, mainly due to some star players who appeared to be entering their prime. As with Giants teams of that era, they played exceptional defense, and offense was always what made Giants fans wary.

The team lost its opening game to their archrivals, the Dallas Cowboys, but then reeled off five straight wins, mostly in games against weak teams in which the Giants played just well enough to win and the defense carried the much-maligned offense to victory. In week six, the team scored 35 points in an uncharacteristic blowout of Philadelphia, and then settled back into their offensive mediocrity with a loss to Seattle and a narrow victory against Washington. Their record stood at 6 wins and 2 losses at midseason, yet Giants fans were their skeptical selves—they would say that the team played great defense every week, but the offense was not explosive enough.

The Giants then ran off five more victories in a row, and a trip to the playoffs was inevitable. Still, though, the concerns persisted about the offense. The "Jints" had scored between 17 and 22 points in each of those last five wins, and it appeared that the team had championship skills on one side of the ball (defense) but not on the other.

However, in the final three games of that 1986 season, with a playoff berth locked up, the Giants' offense seemed to start clicking. It was as if they had made it through the toughest battles of the regular season and the light at the end of the tunnel (Lincoln, Holland, take your pick) was now right in front of them. In week 14 they scored a 10-point victory, and then won by a whopping 20 points in week 15, beating St. Louis by the score of 27-7.

Week 16 came, and observers wondered if the Giants could again muster up enough offense to finish the season 14-2 and clinch home field advantage for the National Football Conference (NFC) playoffs. The team answered that concern with an unlikely 55-24 blowout win over Green Bay to do just that.

The playoffs started with a home game against the vaunted San Francisco 49ers, a powerhouse team at the time. The Giants caught an early break (extra points if you can remember how!) and simply blew away their visitors, 49-3. The team that seemed to have little offensive power had put up 104 points in two games. In the NFC

Championship Game, the "G-Men" shut out Washington, 17-0, and by doing so, made it to the Super Bowl for the very first time. I was a recent college grad, watching the game with my father, and I still remember him jumping up and yelling, "We're going to the Super Bowl!!," and then realizing he meant that the team was going, but we were not.

The Giants, that all-defense, no-offense team that seemingly could not score enough points to be a true championship contender, put up plenty in defeating Denver, 39-20, to win the Super Bowl. In the end, the offense had more than their fair share of the contribution to the team's best season in decades.

So, what's the point of all of this? Think about how the Giants were characterized during much of the regular season. They won week after week, but there was a "show-me" attitude that surrounded the team. As I recall, many fans thought that no matter how good the defense was, the offense would never be able to muster enough week after week to go all the way. Now, let's relate this to some bottom-line points about investor behavior that remind me of fan and media behavior back in 1986.

- *Conclusion 1: Playing good defense is critical to winning championships.* Championship football teams do an outstanding job keeping their team from falling too far behind in a game and in a season. We think investing is that way, too, and I fear that the lessons of this from 2008 may soon be lost if the investor reeducation process does not plow forward, regardless of what current market conditions are at any point in time. As I noted earlier, if you started 2008 with $100, lost $40, leaving you with $60 at year-end, then made 25 percent in 2009 (about what the S&P 500 Total Return gained that year), you are still only back to $75. The subsequent climb after a fall, and the achievement of long-term investment success is much, much tougher if you don't play good defense!
- *Conclusion 2: Modest offense is not necessarily an enduring condition.* I can't tell you in detail what caused the Giants' offense to perk up that season, but I do know that in the past, investors have suffered from what I call the "dangers of extrapolation." This is when you take the current conditions and assume they will continue out into the future. People who did this in early 2000 (and they did so in large numbers) were left holding the

bag. The same thing happened in 2007, when the familiar cry was real estate "can't drop in price" and that consumer leverage was a natural and beautiful thing, not for us to be concerned about—unless you didn't have enough of it. That turned out to be a woefully inaccurate and costly stance for many Americans to take. If you are a financial advisor, don't let this happen to you and your clients again!

If an investment is experiencing lagging performance in a bull market, it could be more a sign of prudent caution than stupidity. If the investment process is as sound as you believed it was when you bought it, don't let short-term underperformance distract you.

Replacing Your Old Investment Playbook (Reprise)

At the beginning of this book, I asked you to turn in your old investment playbook. That is, I wanted you to enter my world of asset allocation with an open mind, and a focus on succeeding for the rest of your investment lifetime. If you made it this far, you have done that. Congratulate yourself!

You now know that this new investment team you have joined emphasizes defense. Their motto is "Defense Wins Championships!" Every investor wants to finish on top—in whatever form that means to them. You now know that your chances of meeting your potential as an investor are much greater if you play excellent defense and have enough offense to win. This is different from trying to outscore the other team with an aggressive attack. In investment parlance, that means don't seek the highest return if it means letting your guard down and taking on too much risk to do so.

Your new investment team runs plays that are different, a bit complex at first, but actually full of common sense. Investment concepts like "low-correlation investing" are not natural to those who were educated in the 1990s mantra of "buy low-cost index funds and hold them." However, you now know that the stock market and bond market are not your friends. They are inanimate objects, filled with many investors with widely varying motives, incentives, and tactics. How do you participate in this "game" without losing your helmet (i.e., your head)? Don't join them! Develop ways to get what you want out of the big sandbox that is Wall Street, and don't believe for a minute that success requires getting beaten up over and over again along the road to success. It doesn't have to. You have to ask yourself why some pro football running backs have long careers while others are done in a few years? The answer, in part, is that the former have a running style that emphasizes avoiding collisions with tacklers. The latter try to run over their tacklers and outmuscle them instead of outmaneuvering them. Both styles can work for a while, but those who use moves instead of muscle have a far better chance of playing longer. And guess what? If you play longer, you make more money! It is the same way in investing. You can't avoid every tackler (i.e., market declines, panic-inducing news, etc.) that the markets send your way. But that doesn't mean you can't try to sidestep a lot of the bruising.

There is more good news from your new team. They have very experienced coaches that work very hard to get you ready for each game. In other words, I have met many financial advisors across the United States who "get" what this book and this investment approach is all about. While their collective voice is small compared to the constant barrage of national TV, web, and print ads issued by their behemoth competitors, their voice is getting louder. I am proud to be one of the "coaches" that helps these forward-thinking advisors prepare their "players" (clients) by equipping them with an approach to win.

Finally, here are the keys to victory for you and me (see Figure 11.3):

1. *Put the right "players" in place for each point in the game.* That is, the investment positioning and repositioning within your portfolio will differ depending on the market environment.
2. *Don't beat ourselves.* Mistakes will happen, losses of capital will occur. That is true for every investor. However, by avoiding most of the common mistakes, you have a far better chance to succeed. Early in this book I identified several of them for you. As the book continued, I reemphasized them, over and over. If I have done my job, many of those themes are now second nature to you.
3. *Mistakes will happen, but avoid big ones.* As you now know, you can do this by incorporating hedging strategies into your portfolio. You don't have to use them all the time, but just having them available for truly uncertain markets can have a greater impact on your returns than any single

•Your new team's motto: Defense Wins
Championships!

•The plays we run: different, a bit complex at
first, but full of common sense (low-correlation
investing)

•Keys to victory:

1. Put the right "players" in place for each point in the game (the styles you
   use).

2. Don't beat ourselves (by making common mistakes).

3. Mistakes will happen, but avoid big ones.

4. Play great "D" and score enough points to win (down-market
   performance is more important than up-market performance).

Figure 11.3   Replacing Your Old Investment Playbook

investment you own. You also now know that low market
correlation, the idea that your portfolio's path diverges
from the broad markets, is another valuable concept to
avoid those big mistakes.

4. *Play great "D" and score enough points to win.* Simply put, down
   market performance is more important than up market performance. Yes, they are both important, but if you don't play
   good defense in your portfolio, you will likely end up being
   part of the herd of investors who unnecessarily force themselves into emotional decisions following dramatic market
   moves. When this happens, it is made worse by the fact that
   millions of other investors are urged on by the media and/or
   are under the influence of Wall Street's enduring culture of
   greed and misdirection (no, not the whole industry, but too
   many of them). This is what happens over and over again during market declines. I have given you, in this book, a detailed
   remedy for that.

The Last Word(s)

Some will say that the investing public, especially in mature stock
markets like the United States, has been hard-wired to believe
that asset allocation means buying long-only stock and bond

mutual funds run by famous portfolio managers, and repeating to yourself, "If I hang in for the long term, it always turns out okay." They will say that Wall Street's education of investors over the past 25 years is too ingrained to reverse itself and open up to modern approaches to asset allocation and portfolio strategy. I respectfully disagree.

I firmly believe that investors are best served by looking beyond traditional approaches to preservation and growth of capital. I am excited to be on the leading edge of my industry's efforts here, and I intend to continue breaking new ground in investment research and portfolio construction. The future will present many challenges for investors, but with a flexible and adaptive asset allocation approach, I believe you can flourish in nearly any market environment and achieve your investment and lifestyle goals whether the market helps you or not.

Perhaps what I have written in this book about how to approach and incorporate the stock market, and how I have practiced asset allocation for many years, will move toward being mainstream thinking during the next decade. I am optimistic about that, since I see changes occurring in my industry every day that affirm such thinking.

Thank you for reading this book. I hope it made you think and added some comfort to the often uncomfortable but critical exercise of properly investing and allocating your assets, now and in the future.

About the Author

Robert A. Isbitts is a Wall Street veteran who began his career in 1986 in New York City. Currently, he is a newsletter writer, published author, and the chief investment officer of an investment management firm. He created and manages the series of investment strategies described in this book, and heads the investment committee that manages them. These strategies are available to wealth managers, financial advisors, and individual investors. He is also the lead manager of an asset allocation mutual fund. Mr. Isbitts was selected by *Worth* magazine as one of the Top 100 Wealth Advisors in the United States in 2005, 2006, 2007, and one of the Top 250 Wealth Advisors in the United States in 2008 by that same publication.

Mr. Isbitts co-founded the investment advisory firm Emerald Asset Advisors in 1998, and prior to that held a variety of portfolio management positions across major institutions such as Fuji Bank Trust, Morgan Stanley, and DLJ. He takes great pride in his efforts to clarify what he believes is an increasingly confusing climate for investors. He writes the *GreenThought$* newsletter and has published more than 100 investment articles and commentaries. His work has been highlighted in several national publications, including *Wealth Manager, Registered Rep, Financial Planning* magazine, *DailyFinance* and *Investment News,* among others. In 2006, Mr. Isbitts' years of research and commentary culminated in the writing of his first book, *Wall Street's Bull and How to Bear It* (Isle Press, 2006). This is his second book.

Mr. Isbitts is a graduate of the State University of New York at Albany, where he earned a degree in business administration in 1986. He earned an MBA in finance from Rutgers University in 1994 and is a Certified Fund Specialist (CFS) designation holder. This advanced training in the analysis and application of mutual funds has served as a strong background for his work in the areas of asset allocation and portfolio management, and was the foundation on which his innovative efforts in this field were built.

Mr. Isbitts and his wife Dana have been married since 1992. They have three children. Mr. Isbitts spends his free time coaching Little League baseball, playing golf, and enjoying the natural beauty of South Florida, his home since 1997.

Mr. Isbitts can be reached directly at rob@flexibleinvesting.net.

Index